CEREAL

CHIP CONRAD

Edited by Denise Chin

This publication is designed to provide accurate and authoritative information in regard to the subject matter covered. It is sold with the understanding that the publisher and author are not engaged in rendering legal, accounting, or other professional advice. If legal advice or other expert assistance is required, the services of a competent professional should be sought.

Copyright © 2016 Chip Conrad

Cover art and design by Nick Pritchett

All rights reserved. No part of this book may be reproduced, stored in a retrieval system, or transmitted by any means, electronic, or otherwise, without written permission from the author, except for the inclusion of brief quotations in review.

ISBN-13:978-1537242453
ISBN-10:1537242458

CONTENTS

PREFACE x
- 1 INTRODUCTION 11
- 2 FAILURE 12
- 3 COWS 13
- 4 MENTORSHIP 14
- 5 THE GAME 14
- 6 JUICE 15
- 7 GIVE 16
- 8 PRIORITIZE 17
- 9 GIVING UP 18
- 10 EMOTIONS 19
- 11 STRENGTH 20
- 12 EMPOWER 21
- 13 EXERCISE 22
- 14 EXCUSES 23
- 15 ADHD 24
- 16 CULTURE 25
- 17 BABIES 26
- 18 MARRIAGE 27
- 19 RAPID-FIRE Q&A 28
- 20 PEPPERMINT 29
- 21 STICKY 30
- 22 PANIC 31
- 23 LUCK 31
- 24 SYSTEMS 32
- 25 DIRECTION 32
- 26 DIRT 33
- 27 NEVER BEHAVE 33
- 28 CHANGE 34
- 29 COMMUNICATION 35
- 30 DONATE 35
- 31 MONEY 36
- 32 ADVICE → SUPPORT 36
- 33 HIRE 37
- 34 CREAM 37
- 35 SMALL SUCCESS 38
- 36 SOCIAL MEDIA 38
- 37 STARTING 39
- 38 COMPETITION 40
- 39 MORE COMPETITION 41
- 40 KILLERS 42
- 41 DIVERSIFY 43
- 42 TOP FIVE STEPS 44
- 43 FRESH EYES 45
- 44 BUSINESS CARDS 45
- 45 TRACK 46
- 46 BUSINESS-SHIP 46
- 47 SCHOOL 47
- 48 EXECUTE 48
- 49 ORIGINAL CONTENT 49
- 50 ADVERTISING 49
- 51 INCUBATE 50
- 52 SOCIAL MEDIA 50
- 53 SMALL BUSINESS 51
- 54 GUTS 51
- 55 WEBSITE 52
- 56 FAKE IT 52
- 57 SOMEBODY ELSE 53
- 58 WOW 54
- 59 TRY HARD 55
- 60 COMMUNITY 56
- 61 KNOWING YOU 57
- 62 KEEP POSTING 58
- 63 INVESTORS 59
- 64 GUERILLA 60
- 65 ENDURANCE 60
- 66 FIT 61
- 67 CONSISTENCY 62
- 68 PACE 63

☐	#	Title	Page		☐	#	Title	Page
☐	69	RESOLUTIONS	63		☐	107	GUT	97
☐	70	KOBE	64		☐	108	FINISH	98
☐	71	SUCCESS	65		☐	109	FIT	98
☐	72	CULTURE	66		☐	110	IGNORANCE	99
☐	73	MOVE	66		☐	111	TRANSPARENCY	100
☐	74	CORK	67		☐	112	HARD	100
☐	75	PERKBIRD	67		☐	113	TEAM	101
☐	76	DRESS	68		☐	114	HIRE	101
☐	77	MEANDER	69		☐	115	FIRE	102
☐	78	FOUR	70		☐	116	TIME	103
☐	79	IDEAS	71		☐	117	GET TESTED	104
☐	80	IRONS	72		☐	118	DIVERSALIZE	105
☐	81	MENTORS	73		☐	119	YOUTHS	106
☐	82	NEGATIVITY	74		☐	120	FILTER	106
☐	83	SERIOUSLY	75		☐	121	PITCH	107
☐	84	MESSED-UPNESSES	76		☐	122	OBJECTION	107
☐	85	PRESSURE	77		☐	123	WORRY	108
☐	86	CELEBRATE	78		☐	124	INFRASTRUCTURE	109
☐	87	EMPLOYEE	79		☐	125	FEAR	110
☐	88	NAPSTER	80		☐	126	TEACH	111
☐	89	SILOS	81		☐	127	GOALS	112
☐	90	SCHOOLS	82		☐	128	GREYISH	112
☐	91	STORY	83		☐	129	R.F.B.	113
☐	92	DEMOGRAPHIC	84		☐	130	PUNCTUAL	114
☐	93	QUESTIONS	85		☐	131	MINIMUN WAGE	114
☐	94	BALANCE	86		☐	132	POLITICS	115
☐	95	MOMENTUM	88		☐	133	THE LINE	116
☐	96	PASSION	89		☐	134	HASTE	117
☐	97	BUSKING	90		☐	135	HELP WANTED	118
☐	98	LOYALTY	91		☐	136	LAUNDRY	119
☐	99	DICK	92		☐	137	FUN	119
☐	100	PREDICTABLE	93		☐	138	FUNNEL	120
☐	101	BUY-IN	93		☐	139	CHARITY	120
☐	102	BE OUTSTANDING	94		☐	140	MR. JONES	121
☐	103	VALUES	95		☐	141	GIVE	122
☐	104	LINE	95		☐	142	BIRTHDAY	123
☐	105	BREATHE	96		☐	143	CHEVETTE	124
☐	106	IGNITION	97					

CEREAL

☐ 145	SHARE	124		☐ 183	UN-ENFUEGO	155
☐ 144	HAPPY	125		☐ 184	MICRO	156
☐ 146	CURRICULUM	126		☐ 185	DOOR	157
☐ 147	UNINSULT	127		☐ 186	VACATION	157
☐ 148	HUSTLEST	127		☐ 187	COMMUNITY	158
☐ 149	STATUS	128		☐ 188	SCALE	159
☐ 150	ERROR	129		☐ 189	PASSION	160
☐ 151	UNLEARN	129		☐ 190	1 YEAR	160
☐ 152	MILLENIALS	130		☐ 191	RE-UP	161
☐ 153	NATIVE	130		☐ 192	LONELY	162
☐ 154	NOW	131		☐ 193	NOT so lonely	163
☐ 155	AMISH	131		☐ 194	F STAGE	164
☐ 156	LINES	132		☐ 195	DRIVE	165
☐ 157	RESPECT	132		☐ 196	LIES	166
☐ 158	SATURN	133		☐ 197	PLAY	167
☐ 159	TWO	134		☐ 198	SURF	168
☐ 160	INNOVATE	135		☐ 199	SURF II	168
☐ 161	VERTS	135		☐ 200	BAD DAYS	169
☐ 162	MANUAL	136		☐ 201	CONSISTENT	169
☐ 163	STAGES	137		☐ 202	FRIENDS	170
☐ 164	SPEND?	138		☐ 203	OVERNIGHT	171
☐ 165	OLD	139		☐ 204	DONE > PERFECT 171	
☐ 166	QUIT	140				
☐ 167	OWNER	141		☐ 205	STRUGGLE	172
☐ 168	80-20	142		☐ 206	WHY NOT	173
☐ 169	YOUT'	143		☐ 207	SHAWSHANK	174
☐ 170	PLAN C	144		☐ 208	THANKS	174
☐ 171	SYNONYMOUS	145		☐ 209	SHOW'EM	175
☐ 172	S&P	146		☐ 210	TEA	176
☐ 173	YES'	147		☐ 211	OUTSTAND	177
☐ 174	10	148		☐ 212	GLENGARRY	178
☐ 175	NO-ING	149		☐ 213	FEELING	179
☐ 176	BOOST	150		☐ 214	MEET	180
☐ 177	PRODUCT	151		☐ 215	SINNOVATION	181
☐ 178	MIDDLE	152		☐ 216	CLICK	181
☐ 179	#1	153		☐ 217	SALSA	182
☐ 180	OUT	153		☐ 218	TEQUILA	183
☐ 181	COMFORT	154		☐ 219	STAND OUT	184
☐ 182	VALUE	154		☐ 220	HAPPY	185

☐ 221	OCEAN	186	☐ 236	KID	199
☐ 222	RUN	186	☐ 237	KODAK	200
☐ 223	FRUIT	187	☐ 238	MEDALS	201
☐ 224	BEACH	188	☐ 239	CONNECTOR	201
☐ 225	WORK	189	☐ 240	BRAVE	202
☐ 226	TIME	190	☐ 241	DRIVE	203
☐ 227	RISK	191	☐ 242	DIGITAL	203
☐ 228	DOUBLE	192	☐ 243	WORK	204
☐ 229	BAND	193	☐ 244	PAPER	205
☐ 230	HEART	193	☐ 245	MARATHON	206
☐ 231	MOVIES	194	☐ 246	NECTAR	206
☐ 232	KAP	195	☐ 247	PRODUCTIVITY	207
☐ 233	IPHONE	196	☐ 248	UNDER-FIRE	207
☐ 234	JET SKI	197	☐ 249	MENTORING	208
☐ 235	TOGETHER	198	☐ 250	NO AND GO	209

For Zoie and Tripp

Follow your dreams.

PREFACE

There was a time in my life when my hobby was to make furniture from used pallet wood. I would build pieces and set the ones I liked somewhere in public for people to use or take. One thing I liked about this hobby was that I didn't try to make these pieces perfect but they were completed and functional.

In the same way, CEREAL is a composition of my experiences. This book is not perfect, polished, or refined. It's completed and functional. It follows my journey for a short time and shows how I have grown as a person and business owner; how my feelings have changed and experiences have moved my paradigm.

Why 250 lessons? Because there are 250 work days in a year, and it is my hope that you use this as a reader for your every work day. I've included a check box for every lesson so you can check them off as you read (and for those of us who just love to check boxes).

CEREAL was written based on content from my daily vlog on entrepreneurship, found on Facebook.com/chipsvlog

☐ 1   INTRODUCTION

Over the years, I've been labeled by other people, and maybe even by myself, as crazy. The other day I was called a cowboy. I don't know exactly what they mean, except maybe that I seem brave for what I do: As a serial entrepreneur, it seems like I spend a lot of my time taking risks, betting it all, doubling down, and—point, shoot, aim!—breaking a lot of things. For the most part they're right. But I've seen how this attitude and approach to business has really paid off, not only in monetary value (which is not much) but in happiness, joy, and fulfillment. I feel that this "cowboy" attitude is something I could pass on not only to my kids and family, but also to other people in general. I spend a lot of time helping people get over what they think are barriers. Turning what they think are walls into just hurdles, or thin walls that you can punch through like the Hawaiian Punch guy.

Here's what I've come to learn: People don't need much advice or encouragement. Most of the time, they just need to be reminded of the things they already know. Recently, I met with a gentleman and we talked for about 45 minutes. I had some okay things to say to him. I felt like he listened to a lot of it, but after that he sent me a text and said, "Chip, thanks for the reminder." I thought I had given him advice on something I knew a lot about. The truth was that he already knew that. He just needed to be reminded.

You're the best of what you do in all that you've already experienced. Your challenges are not walls, they are just hurdles. If they are walls, they are thinner than you think.

☐ 2 FAILURE

I was in a meeting with a client who was quite shocked that I had used the word failure. I was recently involved in a program where we missed some of our goals; we didn't really hit what we were looking for, and to me that was a failure.

I find that people sometimes want to turn the word failure into something more positive. They say, "No, it's just an issue" or "We were just trying something", when really, failure is the right word for it. I like the word failure because it's a bit shocking and I think that's what failure should do—shock.

Failure should be like getting hit by a Mack truck made of nerf. (I feel that if you got hit by a real Mack truck you'd probably die) It should be violent. You should also get back up as quickly as possible and learn from it.

In my life I've had failures and successes. I usually learn more by failing than winning. Failure is when you set a goal and you don't reach that goal. Own your failures as much as you own your successes.

There are three different ways you should fail. Preferably, mix them all together:

1. **You should fail fast**

    Failing fast allows you to get up and get back on the horse and learn from the mistake that you made.

2. **You should fail hard**

    Failing hard means that you went for it. Tiny failures are no fun. They're annoying. If you're going to go for it, go for it. Go big or go home. Fail hard. Fail big. All the most successful people in this world have failed. As a matter of fact, they mostly failed and failed hard.

3. **You should fail publicly**

The worst thing to do is watch a funny movie by yourself because you want to laugh out loud and show everybody what you think is funny. In the same way, when you're failing and you're really going for it, you should let those around you know. Family, friends, associates, acquaintances, the general public, because when you do fail they're there to laugh with you. You can laugh at the parts of the failure that you find funny, which will be most of it.

☐ 3 COWS

As a small business owner, you tend to play lots of roles within your company. One of the roles I want to talk about today is the role of salesman. It's an important skill that Starters have to learn, either the easy way or the hard way. When I was starting my first company, I rode in the back of a 15-passenger van on a cell phone about the size of a hoagie sandwich, booking my comedy troupe as we were on tour.

A trick I learned was to not set sales goals but set sales CALL goals.

There were warm leads, people that I have contacted from a cold call that eventually said something other than, "No." Then there were cold calls, straight up cold calls. I would set a goal of 20 calls in one day, instead of focusing on the number of sales. This sometimes didn't equal to any sale, but sometimes it amounted to many sales. Sales are unicorns. You just never know when they're going to show up. Cold calls are cows. They show up everywhere, all the time, and sometimes they're super annoying.

I set my goals this way because the amount of calls I could make was tangible. The amount of sales that I could get was not.

My encouragement for today is to make sure you set your sales goals on something that's tangible, not something you have no control over.

☐ 4   MENTORSHIP

I don't know yet if being a mentor or a mentee has more impact on a person. I've found that I learn more when I've walked with somebody through their struggles and by being there for them, than when somebody was giving me advice. So being a mentor to somebody is better than mentee, I would think. Make yourself available. Search for those opportunities, and learn from it.

☐ 5   THE GAME

"The first step to winning the game is admitting that there is one."
- Unknown

About three years ago, I started swimming three times a week because of an injury I had in my neck. Then I really got addicted to it, and I now do it a lot. It makes me feel good, not while I'm doing it, but after I've done it. One thing I noticed is that if I'm in a lane swimming, and if you're in either of the lanes also swimming—if we start our lap at the same time, it becomes my goal to beat you back on that lap. No matter what I do, I still feel the urge to beat you to the other side of the pool, even though you're doing your workout, and I'm doing mine. I don't know you from Adam.

I think that's what it's like to be a business owner, whether small or large business, in the community. The game is there. Sometimes it's really evident whom that game is with, and sometimes it's not. It's pretty ambiguous. The game is always there. The best entrepreneurs are small business owners who are not motivated by money. Read any of Tony Hsieh's books. It's not the money that he does this for; it's for the game.

☐ 6   JUICE

It's really hard to show that you're hustling by saying, "Look at the hours I've worked!" I look back and think, "Well, was I efficient? Are the systems I have in place allowing me to work efficiently? Was most of that time spent watching YouTube videos?"

Am I doing all I can to really get the most out of work? Family comes first all the time, so if you juice work time, then you really get to juice family time correctly. Get work done while you're being efficient. Strike while the iron is hot.

My challenge for you is to take a look at the hours you're working. Are you really juicing the work out of your work time? That being said, sometimes you really do need to go watch a YouTube video. Sometimes you need to unplug, disconnect, take a walk, change desk, stand up, sit down, or call your family to get that working brain clicking back on.

☐ 7   GIVE

I don't know if you know what Rotary is, but it's a group focused on servicing the community and other communities. It's usually filled with men over the age of 60, but in most circumstances they're very helpful to the community.

Lots of people join the Chamber of Commerce, or BMI, or PNI, or networking groups expecting something to happen for them immediately. This is the wrong way to approach a community group, service group, or networking group. The right way is to join the group and ask what you can do for the group. Ask not what your group can do for you, but what you can do for your group.

The best small business owners are those whose first instinct is to serve the group they're joining, not to ask somebody for something. You can't ask for something until you give, and give a lot. Of course you want to grow your business. Everybody wants to grow their business. You want to be seen as being involved in the community. So does everybody. The ones who truly shine, who stand out, are the ones who serve first. Serve first, second, and third, then ask.

Serve for a good, long time. If you do, in the end, you might not even have to ask for anything. When you build a reputation for yourself as somebody who wants to serve, people will ask you about your business. They will patronize your business. It's a backwards concept, because everybody knows we're all just trying to grow our business. Give first, second, and third, before you ask.

☐ 8 PRIORITIZE

Work in circles.

Here's how my day usually goes—emails, phone calls, tasks. It usually circulates like that, emails, phone calls, tasks.

First, emails. One thing I've realized about dealing with customers and clients is that the quicker your response, the more forgiving they are of your brevity or spelling/grammar errors. In other words, if a client writes you a two-paragraph question and you answer within minutes of getting the email with a one-liner that answers their question, they're happy with that. If their email sat in your inbox all day and you answer with a one-liner, they get upset.

Next are texts. Clients, friends, family are all becoming more tolerant of texts. It has a quicker response time than phone calls and allows the recipient to get to it when they can. I've gone to the point of telling people, on my outgoing voice mail message, to text me if I missed their call.

For people in sales only:

Make call to leads and return voice messages.

I use a task list called Wunderlist. It helps me prioritize, pick up, drag, drop. I prioritize my tasks according to money—which of these tasks equal money, and the largest amounts of money? Largest amounts of money tasks get done first. CREAM.

If there's no money involved, I do the hardest task first. If you're not doing your hardest task first then change; it's the only way to prioritize.

9 GIVING UP

Recently, my 6-year-old taught me something about giving up. Zoie decided to go to swim camp this summer, which is not really a camp as much as it is one hour out of a day, five days a week, going and learning how to swim. She did amazingly. In this swim class, what they want you to do is level up. You begin swimming with simple challenges, and then when your instructor decides that you're ready, another swim instructor comes over and watches you do these techniques. If you've to learned these techniques, you level up again, and again, until you finish.

On the last day of swim camp, Zoie really wanted get to the final level. She was so determined to do that. But at the end of the final day, she failed to hit the last level. That was it. Zoie got out of the water and held it together on her way walking over to me and her mom where we were sitting. As she got to us she broke down, started crying, and was inconsolable. As a father, I was distraught. My heart was really broken for her. My son was with me, so my daughter and wife decided to go into the hot tub to take a breather and calm down (Zoie doesn't like to cry around people). My son and I decided to walk around and see what the aquatic center had to offer.

When we came back to the pool area, I was surprised to see that my daughter had gone to get her instructor and the head instructor. She had convinced them to come back because she was determined to level up. And she made it to the final level, on the final day.

There are times when you feel that you just can't go on. You don't think there's any more left in your tank and all you want to do is go to a corner and cry. This is fine, but what's important is that after we're done crying, we go back and get the instructor. We pull them over to the pool and decide to level up.

CEREAL

☐ 10   EMOTIONS

Have you ever heard the story about Michael Jackson and Paul McCartney? Paul McCartney and Michael Jackson at one time were very good friends. Until Michael Jackson purchased the rights to every Beatle song ever recorded. He was so filthy, dirty, stinking rich. This made Paul McCartney very upset with Michael Jackson. "It's just a business decision, Paul. We're still friends, but business is business. This is a wise investment," Michael said. That's similar to this analogy: Picture your best friend, picture your business. Imagine your best friend buying the building your business is in and raising the rent.

I've thought about this story at different chapters of my life. In my current chapter, I'm more impressed by that story than ever. Emotions have very little to do with your business. You should not make business decisions emotionally. "I want to fire this person because this person made me mad," is a perfect example. If you make that decision emotionally, it might hurt your business professionally because the person you were just about to fire might be very good for your business.

Emotions should be taken out of your business decisions. Michael Jackson was right. "It's just a business decision, Paul." Emotions and business—never mix them. Listen to Michael Jackson.

☐ 11 STRENGTH

I love being an entrepreneur way better than having a miserable job. Not to say that being a starter and business owner is not miserable. There are times when it's miserable, but the fact that you're doing something you love makes it all worth it. When starting a new thing, I've had a lot of people say, "Oh Chip, a new thing. Chip's doing a new thing." Followed by eye rolling. Referring to it like it is a weakness, or a disability.

I just want to encourage anybody out there who has a reputation for being a starter and is willing to work 80 hours a week to make nothing from a job you love, as opposed to working 40 hours a week and making $100,000 a year at a job you hate. I'm telling you that that trait is not a weakness. Don't let people pat you on the head and say, "That's just our little girl," or "That's just our little boy, starting ANOTHER company." Everybody's going to pat you on the head and look down at you, until you achieve what they think is success.

Shoot for what you feel is success, because you've been granted this opportunity to be able to do what you want. It's not a disability; it's a strength. If you're a starter, a small business owner, an entrepreneur, or a risk-taker, don't let anybody treat you like those things are weaknesses, because they're strengths, and they are strengths that our nation, and even mankind, depend on.

☐ 12   EMPOWER

"I have to bring this back to the comedy club, otherwise my staff is going to yell at me," I said as I returned a shopping cart used to load goods. I think some people might read that and think, "That's kind of backwards. You're the owner, why is your staff yelling at you?"

I think you should always be working your way out of your position. As a small business owner, you should always be training people to take your spot.

On day one, when I started my comedy club, I was the leader, the guy needed, the guy that was everywhere, the guy that did everything. As time passed, I was still the leader, but I was not very needed. You should always be empowering your employees. You should always be training somebody to take your spot. If you are the person in your company who, after five years, is still doing the majority of your work, depending on what industry or what business it is, then that is a terrible loss for you. People around you are often more capable of doing the day-to-day tasks than you are.

You, as a business owner, are probably only good at two or three things. The rest need to be done by people who are better than you at that task.

Now let's take this shopping cart back.

☐ 13 EXERCISE

The positive effects that exercise can have on your mental health is no secret, therefore, exercising regularly is going to make you a better small business owner. The problem is that we're too busy. We are in back-to-back meetings all day and then we have a family that we run all night. It doesn't leave much time for us to exercise.

Here's what I try and do: I started scheduling workouts as if they were meetings. When anybody asked for a meeting during my exercise time slot, I would say, "No, I have a meeting." They don't need to know that it's for working out.

You might say, "You're just working out. That's not a meeting. That's not as important." But it *is* important. Physical exercise is really important. It helps you be better at your job as a small business owner. Just like conventions and seminars—it's that important. If you're going to conferences, seminars, or trainings to sharpen your skills, then you should also be booking regularly scheduled times for workouts.

Make sure that you're booking your exercise times as appointments and you won't leave out exercise.

☐ 14 EXCUSES

While golfing with a gentleman, we got to talking about what we did for work. He asked me what I do, and I gave him my typical answer. Then I asked him what he did and he told me, rather monotonously. Then I asked him what his dream was, and his face just lit up.

For me, if you love your job, and if that doesn't involve starting your own company, you're happy there, you're fulfilled, and you get joy from it, then great. That's your thing. That's fine. What I do have a problem with in a lot of people is that they don't like their job, but they feel like they have to do it. Then they say what their dream is, but follow up with, "Yeah, but I got this, and then I got that, and this is a problem, and that's a problem, so there's no way I could ever blah blah blah blah blah."

They say that the number one reason small businesses fail is lack of funding, but I'm going challenge that. I think the number one reason that small businesses fail is because of excuses. Nationwide, the largest killer of small businesses is those damn excuses. Stop making excuses and build the job of your dreams. It's the hardest thing you'll ever do, but it will be well worth it.

Do what you want to do for a living. Stop making excuses. Start working towards your dreams. Everybody around you will be happier.

☐ 15   ADHD

I feel led today to talk about a disease that a lot of entrepreneurs, small business owners, and leaders have but isn't addressed enough. It is something I suffer from as well. The disease is called Attention Deficit Hyperactivity Disorder (ADHD).

There are all kinds of forms of this disease. It can take many different shapes, but there is stunning information out there about people with ADHD being good business starters, leaders, builders, and so on. So there's very much a positive side to it, but there is just as much of a bad side. Sometimes it comes with issues like dyslexia, hyperactivity, and anxiety, among others, and I find that a lot of people discredit these or laugh them off. Sometimes they use these as an excuse in life. OR sometimes they don't know that they have it and they're wondering why they're having issues. My encouragement today is to those of you who have ADHD, think you have ADHD, or are running into issues and you don't know why, I would encourage all three of those groups of people to get tested for ADHD.

Find out where you are on the scale so that you can better navigate your way through you life and your small business.

16 CULTURE

A friend of mine, Fred Hollow, asked, "How do you translate, "That's a really cool idea" into "That's a really cool idea and here's some money for your product"?" Here's a little bit about Fred. Fred has a product that he sells called Nuvo Glass. It's cool. What he does is he upcycles wine and liquor bottles by doing something secret to them, and then turns them into bowls and glasses. His products look really cool and are amazing.

See, I just did it there. This is exactly what he's saying. How do you convert people around you to say, "Wow, that's such a cool product. Here's money for that product"?

Firstly, your product is cool, you got that going for you. The culture of your company needs to be cool too. People who want to give you money for your product want to know that they're joining something bigger than just buying a product. This is why Dutch Bros., one of my favorite drive-through coffee companies here in the Northwest, is big. When I buy at Dutch Bros., it's liquid with sugar and caffeine in it. But really, having a cup of coffee from Dutch Bros. says something more than just that you bought something from them; it says you joined their tribe and you're part of their movement.

Dutch Bros. understands that the only thing you can have proprietary to a coffee business is your culture. Anybody can put coffee in a filter and run water through it and put it in a cup. Hardly anybody can create a culture like Dutch Bros. has. Create a culture with your company. You already have a really cool product, now start a really cool culture.

☐ 17   BABIES

Businesses are a lot like babies. There's good and bad. The bad is that they annoy you sometimes, and they keep you up at night. Sometimes they poop on your shirt. There are good things. You fall in love with them, they're amazing, they look and feel and smell like you. They're incredible. They become the loves of your life. They become the one of the things you would die for.

Know that when you meet a business owner, their business is their baby. There's a bad side that not a lot of business owners have to come to and that is eventually having to say goodbye to your business. When you see a business owner having to say goodbye to their business, know that that is one of the saddest days of their life.

Customers: The next time you're in a business, know that that's someone's baby and treat it with care.

Business owners: Know that some day you will say goodbye to you business and make sure you think about that day a lot.

☐ 18   MARRIAGE

Guys, do you remember that girl in high school your buddy started dating and at first glance you were like, "I don't know what he sees in her." Then you meet her and you're like, "Oh man. Wow." Then you do all you can to steal her away. Ladies, I'm sure a similar situation happens with you, although probably a little differently.

That girl/guy is an illustration of a business that doesn't have the best website, signs out front, maybe is a little bit dirty, but once you get to know that business, you are in love. All the fluffy stuff doesn't matter anymore.

The other is a very "pretty" business. Remember this guy/girl? You see them. You're like, "Whoa. I want him. He's a 10. I love what I see. I want him." Then you get to know them and they start sliding down the scale because they're all about themself. They don't like anything outside of Forever 21 or video games, but they're attractive and they have your interest.

The third way is like my wife, or your own significant other. Super hot and a very deep thinker. You just want to be around them. Attractive on all fronts. My wife literally has a line of people wanting to spend time with her. This is the reason I tricked her into marrying me. Marriage material!

So, there are three ways to market your company:

1. There's the person you want to steal from your buddy because initially, you didn't see what they saw, but then you fell in love with them.

2. There's the girl or guy who was really hot and then the connection was shallow.

3. Then there are businesses a lot like our significant others, who are super hot, and then also super deep. Marriage material.

Is your business marriage material?

☐ 19   RAPID-FIRE Q&A

Alright, time for Q&A. Here we go. I'm answering them rapid-fire.

Question: When my socks disappear in the dryer, where do they go?

Answer: Hell.

Question: Nonprofit or for-profit? What are the pros and cons of both, and how to know which is best for your own aspirations?

Answer: Stay away from nonprofits as much as you possibly can. Starting a nonprofit should be your last resort. Go to nonprofit if it's a charitable cause and you know a really good grant-writer.

Question: What has been your greatest inspiration?

Answer: YouTube videos

Question: a) What is the meaning of life?
b) Why does every entrepreneur need to know their why?

Answer: a) The meaning of life is love.
b) So they have a reason to get up in the morning, or else they'll just stay in bed all day.

Question: Why grammar is important?

Answer: I see what you're saying here. So that you can make people feel terrible when you correct them with "who" or "whom."

Question: What is the most effective and inspirational business book you've read in the past year?

Answer: I don't read books. I listen to them, and nothing inspirational this year.

Question: What is the 83rd digit of pi?

Answer: Hold on, carry the 1...I don't know.

☐ 20 PEPPERMINT

As small business owners, we provide a product or a service. Sometimes we can get ahead of ourselves by assuming that the customer wants our product or service the way we want to give it to them. Say I have an ice cream store and my customer comes in and says, "I want peppermint-flavored ice cream." We walk over to the peppermint-flavored ice cream and we scoop it out and we give it to them. Then that customer says, "This is not peppermint. I wanted peppermint." Our first reaction as small business owners is to point at the peppermint label and say, "No, that's peppermint. I gave you peppermint."

Let's let our knee-jerk reaction as small business owners be, "Well what is your interpretation of peppermint?" Maybe their interpretation of peppermint is vanilla. It's just that they've called vanilla ice cream peppermint their whole life. It's our job as small business owners to give our customers exactly what they want, even if their idea of what they want is different from ours.

☐ 21   STICKY

I while back I ran into a couple of people I know. They were with a few other people that I didn't know very well. My friend stated, "Chip vlogs about this thing that's coming," to which they replied, "What's the thing?" I said, "I can't tell you. I'm not telling anybody."

"How do you expect to draw attention to your new business if you don't tell anybody what it is?" they asked. I didn't respond, and right away, one of them spoke up and said, "We're talking about it now, aren't we?" I knew that if I didn't tell them what it was they would think about that conversation all day, whereas if I had just told them what it was, this would have just been passing conversation. What I did stuck in their minds. I was being sticky.

Here are examples of non-sticky marketing: A basic ad in a newspaper, a commercial on cable, a Facebook post. A lot of marketing is not very sticky, but there has to be sticky points to it (it can't be a discount or sale). We, as humans, get ad blindness very easily.

Think about your marketing. Are there sticky points to your marketing? Are you sticky?

☐ 22   PANIC

One thing I've learned over the years as a business owner is that you have to learn to be unreactionary (I made that word up). What I mean is, you have to learn to be even-keeled. I really find that it doesn't do any good to panic.

Here's why: Sometimes you stumble across something that will make you want to freak out, and either you do or you don't, but in the long run, you find out that that wasn't worth freaking out about. Things are never as bad or as good as they seem. That's just a fact. So when you're faced with a challenge or something unexpected in your business, it does no good to panic. Just chill. You don't have a boss, so any day without a boss is better than any day with a boss.

☐ 23   LUCK

I don't claim to know a lot about business, I just claim to know a lot about things I've failed at and then learned from. The success of your business sometimes has a lot to do with luck and timing. I'm not taking anything away from hard work. Bon Jovi says the harder we work the luckier we get—I truly believe in that.

I'm not saying this so that you sit back and wait for timing, and/or for luck; I say it so that if your business is struggling right now, or if it's not getting off the ground, it might not be because of your skills—it might be because the timing's just not right yet. Keep working hard. Keep pushing through. Work long. Work hard. You'll get there eventually. I promise.

☐ 24   SYSTEMS

I paid a visit to Oil Can Henry's the other day. "Oil Can Henry's" should be an adjective. Let me tell you why. Everything—from how they hire to what they wear and what they do—is all planned. This makes their service highly predictable. The system works.

Systems leave little room for mistakes. Hat. Bow tie. Shirt. Jacket. Stick to the script. What McDonald's has done to burgers, Oil Can Henry's has done to the oil change industry. Have you Oil Can Henry'd your business?

Integrate systems, be predictable, attract customers.

☐ 25   DIRECTION

Set a goal, make a plan, work the plan, achieve the goal. I've done all of that at least once in my life but I think a lot of people get hung up on the business plan. I don't like business plans because they turn people off, not initially but definitely after they don't achieve their plan. I think the better word for business plan should be your business "direction".

A plan is like, "This is the route we are going to take." Well, shit happens, and when it happens to new business owners, it turns them off, and then they go back to their day job. I'm changing the term "business plan" to "business direction".

Here is what you should do: Got an idea for a business? Write a business plan. Make it huge. Make it awesome. Make it extend five years out with a corporate buyout. Go nuts! DREAM! Do that, but make another plan a month in and throw the old one away and keep doing that each month, or each quarter if you are lazy. This will keep you from getting discouraged when you are not profitable in the first two months. If you are on target, you are hitting your milestones, don't change it.

☐ 26   DIRT

I thought of a good analogy for what it's like to be an entrepreneur. Picture a tree with one apple hanging from it. That's what you want, but you can't get to that apple so you need to build a mound of dirt so that you can walk up the dirt and get to that apple.

Being an entrepreneur is like digging a hole and then asking people to come throw dirt in it until eventually, you're up to where you started. And then since you've asked so many people to throw dirt in the hole, people keep coming and it eventually starts to stack up. At some point you finally get that apple.

☐ 27   NEVER BEHAVE

My friend Rebecca is taking portable toilets, decorating them artistically and placing them in our community for the homeless to use. Genius!

She said, "I told you guys, I can't behave." That is such a great statement. If you're going to behave, go get a desk job. We need more people who aren't going behave, people who are going to push the envelope, not listen to others, the rules, or what your parents told you.

Paving new paths, that's what we need. Never behave.

☐ 28   CHANGE

Two friends asked me similar questions last night:

"How do you see small business changing in the next five years?"

"How are you going to deal with the changes coming to small business?"

There are some things that will never change in the service industry—really good customer service will always trump everything.

What will change? Connectivity. How people find your business. How people talk about your business. That's going to become easier in the future. The way people engage with your business is going to change very rapidly. The way you advertise has already changed, and it's going to keep changing.

I think the people who are going to win with that change are those who are authentic, who open up their business in every angle for people to see; the people that build relationships and show vulnerability. I think they're going to win because people are going to be able to read their story more easily. If you can tell your story better in the next five years, you will win. That's how I see it changing.

☐ 29 COMMUNICATION

Here's a question regarding managing people: "What habit do you have that negatively affects your team, and what do you do to counteract it?"

My worst habit is that I am not a communicator. My team calls it the Chip chip. People who work well with Chip have a chip in their brain that is from me. I telepathically tell them what to do and they figure it out, which means people who take the initiative and those who don't need much guidance usually work very well with me.

Even with that said, my worst habit still is not communicating enough. What do I do to counteract it? I usually over communicate. It seems like I'm over communicating in my head but to my employees and team members, I'm not, I'm just being normal at communicating. I don't have a lot of need to communicate, so I have to over-compensate for that when I'm dealing with my team. You?

☐ 30 DONATE

Make sure you're giving back to your community. A good healthy community will lay a solid foundation for a successful business.

For me, I fund whichever non-profit is doing something I wish I could run myself. Mostly, these are organizations that deal with underserved youth.

I give to an organization called Family Building Blocks. Organizations like these resonate with people who have kids. They train parents on how to be good parents, and that is awesome.

☐ 31 MONEY

"How do I get grants or investments without giving away most of my company?"

Fund it yourself, apply for a line of credit, or save up for a long time and throw all of that hard-earned cash into it. There's really no way of raising capital without giving some of it, if not a lot of it, away.

That's the name of the game. You're the idea, if you're lucky you can execute and money is the crux. If you don't have money, you can't do the rest. You've got to give part of the company away. Just figure that into the grand plan. Play the long game. Start it, build it, grow it, sell it.

☐ 32 ADVICE → SUPPORT

"Hey, I wonder what you think about my product?" or "Will you buy my product?"

Sales are a matter of going through as many "no's" as it takes to get to that "yes". When you're done getting maybes and you need that full "no" or that full "yes", that's when you switch over to say, "Alright buddy, are you going to give me money for this or not?"

That's when you switch from advice to support.

☐ 33   HIRE

"How do I handle paperwork?"

Paperwork is a lot of entrepreneurs' enemy. Us, entrepreneurs, we are ADHD, we are dyslexic, we are impulsive, we are not very detail-oriented—that is a fact.

Hire somebody to do it. Hiring people at a fair wage to do the things that you aren't good at is always worth it for you. You'll spend way more time doing the things that you are good at, which in turn will make you more money, and in turn give you more funds to hire people to do the thing that you can't do.

Take the risk, bite off a little bit, hire them for a couple of hours at first, then a couple of days at first, and then finally work your way up. That's a way to make it affordable. You will see the change immediately and you will enjoy it, I guarantee it.

☐ 34   CREAM

"Does it really take money to make money?"

Easy answer? Yes. Not so easy answer? Kind of. I say that because I've built three companies from the ground up at this point and all of them took very little money.

I actually have a really funny story about that. I used to travel doing comedy with a guy, lets call him Hank. After every show, we used to have a place where you could buy merchandise. We didn't have a sign; we just had our merchandise sitting there. One day Hank came to me and said, "I think we should have a sign that says, "Isaac Improv"," and I said, "I don't know, we don't really have the money." He said, "Chip, it takes money to make money." So we got the sign and used it. Once. Then he left it at a location and we didn't go back to get it.

I don't know what you could gain from that story, but yes, it does take money to make money.

☐ 35 SMALL SUCCESS

"Is it possible to be hyper-small and achieve success?"

Success means a lot of things to different people. If you're talking about monetary success, it's pretty much impossible to make a lot of money when you're super small—I mean, if we're talking millions of dollars. Business has to scale.

On the other hand, if you're talking about success in having enough money to live, and being happy, and doing something you love, there's a phrase, "Stay small, and keep it all." That's keeping to the idea of not hiring too many people, "I do them well enough and I can manage, so I don't have to pay out any money."

It just depends on how you define success. I define success by being happy and loving what I do. Money is a byproduct. Not very many entrepreneurs are monetarily driven; it's the game that drives them.

So yeah, if you want to make a lot of money, you have to scale. You can't stay small. If you want to make a good amount of money and be super happy, absolutely possible. Stay small, keep it all.

☐ 36 SOCIAL MEDIA

"How important is social media to your company, in terms of marketing?"

Very important. Super-duper important. As important as the newspaper was in the 80s. As important as the yellow pages were in the 70s. As important as braille in the dark ages.

I really feel that with the way things are going, pretty soon when we talk about marketing, it's going to be understood that we are mostly talking about social media. We're all going digital. Here's what I'm saying—social media is super important. Advertising is all about eyeballs, and everybody's eyeballs are on social media. Get in there, figure it out.

☐ 37 STARTING

"Where do I start when starting a business, regarding license and L.L.C.?"

This is half the problem.

I had a meeting last week with a gentleman who's running for governor of Oregon, and he said, "What is the one thing that you would like to change about starting a small business in Oregon?"

I said to him, "There needs to be one webpage that you go to and it says, "Do you want to start a business? Yes or no?" And then you click on one of the buttons and from there it goes to another set of questions. You should be able to work your way through the whole process until you have your company started legally by authority of the government, set up and ready to go. So many people want to start businesses but don't know how to. They get stuck somewhere, or they start a business and God forbid, they do something wrong, and they get sued or fined right off the bat."

Here's how I started my businesses. I never applied for a business license. I went to the state, registered the name, I went to Legal Zoom, and I opened up an L.L.C. Have I made a bunch of mistakes along the way because there aren't a lot of resources out there for regular Americans to start a company? Yes. Most definitely. Will that change? I hope so.

☐ 38   COMPETITION

My first rule about competition is that if you're afraid of it, then your product or service isn't as good as you'd like it to be. When I owned a comedy club, there were other venues in town that brought in comedy, but we were not worried about the competition, because we knew that we were the best at what we did. My team knew that. That is the culture we built in our club. If you're confident and you know that, then competition does nothing but shine a light on how good your product or service is.

That being said, competition moves your whole industry forward. There's a study I read recently that showed that the more co-working spaces there are in a city, the more likely those co-working spaces are to succeed. I think the reason is because together, you and your competitors move in that industry, like a flock of geese. When they fly together, they all fly faster. I guarantee some of those geese are racing each other. That's a guarantee. Geese race each other.

Secondly, anytime you can network with someone in your industry, that does nothing but help the both of you. I freely share everything I know about the comedy industry with anyone who wants to know, because we're all going to move forward. If another comedy club opens up in Salem, I would be super happy about that, because you're just bringing more awareness to the importance of having laughter in your community.

If you're worried about competition, your product or service is not as good as you'd like it to be.

☐ 39 MORE COMPETITION

"How much time and attention should you designate to analyze the competition?"

How much time do race car drivers spend looking in the rear view mirror? Probably not much. If they spend too much time not looking ahead, they're going to run into somebody. If you're worried about competition, you're not very confident with your product or service. For me, I like to band together with competition. A high tide raises all boats.

Suffice to say, I don't spend much time, and I don't think you should spend much time, analyzing competition. Are you the best? As long as you're the best, there's no reason to look at the competition. Share ideas with the competition, band together. If you're afraid of competition, that's a bad place to be.

☐ 40   KILLERS

"What are the top five mistakes that business owners make when they start their business, or that new business owners make?"

I decided to name these after movies. We're going to go from five to one.

5. Top Gun

It's all about them. They start their business. All they ever do is talk and push their business, make Facebook and Twitter updates. They don't talk about how they can help the community around their business grow.

4. Cast Away

These are the guys that get out there and say, "I can do it all myself. I don't need any help. I don't need somebody on payroll. I don't need anybody's input or answers." They do it all alone. They don't want to listen to anybody, or take any advice, but they go for it.

3. Lost Boys

When it comes to branding, they piece it all together, this from here, that from there—the Lost Boy fonts of 1980, Lost Boy logos from my uncle, and the Lost Boy WordPress template and website—and they build it all up. It's all pieced and mashed together. It's lost.

2. Field of Dreams

This pertains to the idea of if you build it, they will come. I see this all the time. They build it. They sit there and they wait for people to come but it never happens. They don't do anything else but build, expecting everybody to come. "I have this great sandwich shop. I'll open it up. Everybody will come in." Then soon you find that nobody does because they don't know about you or because you used your uncle's logo (refer to #3).

1. Failure to launch

This is the number one killer of small business in America. The idea that's still in your head that you failed to try. Get out there and start a business. Today is the day.

☐ 41   DIVERSIFY

A friend, a professional pressure washer, asked, "What can I do as a side gig during the winter when there's not a lot to wash?"

Diversify. When I ran a comedy club, we made money by adding beer and wine to our menu, events, and remote shows. Look inside the container of your business. What other streams of revenue can you make with what you have in that container?

When I shaped surfboards in San Diego, I read an article about people inland riding boat wakes, so I started making wake-surfers. Introducing other lines of revenue into your business is a very good idea.

Do something that keeps you around your target customers. This will keep you on top-of-mind with them.

42 TOP FIVE STEPS

"What are the five first steps of creating your own business?"

1. Make sure you have a passion for what you're doing

Passion will trump everything. If you don't have passion for it, you will fail. Money is not enough of a driving factor. You might have a passion for money and that passion is your driving factor, not money.

2. Time equals money

Money is time. If you don't have money to hire somebody to do the things that are necessary to starting a business, you better have time to figure out how to do it yourself. Make sure you have enough cash or enough time. Time is money. Cash is oxygen for business.

3. Support

Moral support. Is there support around you? Do you have the people that are closest to you that are in favor of what you're doing? That's going to help out a lot. If you don't have that, it's going to be pretty hard. You need to surround yourself with people who are supportive of what you're going to do.

4. Proof of Concept (POC)

The fourth most important thing when starting a business is making sure that what you are doing is going to make money. You have to make sure that your concept has proof that it will work.

5. Know your strengths

Find out what you do well. It's probably going to be about two or three things. Surround yourself with people who can do all the other things in business better than you can. That will give you a good jumpstart on succeeding in your business.

☐ 43   FRESH EYES

"How important is it for a business owner to stay a beginner? In other words, for a business owner to see their business through the eyes of their customers?"

It's important that we don't tell our customers how to use our product or service. I mean, unless we're Apple. And nobody's Apple, really. Customers will tell you exactly how they want to be dealt with. Anytime you can, get data from fresh eyes. Either get it from somebody else, or find ways to get you to have fresh eyes on your business. Get some fresh eyes on your business.

☐ 44   BUSINESS CARDS

"Are printed business cards still a worthwhile instrument for your business?"

Such a great question, I'm so glad you asked. With a printed business card, all you're doing is saying here's a piece of paper, it's going to sit on your nightstand or you're going to file it away in some drawer where you put all this other stuff...You're causing you just met to do all of this because you were too lazy to go, "Hey, what's your number?" You're putting that on them.

In business, if your game still involves handing somebody a business card, then your game is whack. Ditch paper. Give your information and take information on your phone, the thing you touch 480,000 times a day.

(Those in sales are exempt from this rule)

☐ 45   TRACK

While I carry the moniker of "biz dev" for most projects I'm on, I don't really consider that as frontline sales. There are only a few people really cut out for frontline sales. For those on the frontlines, I recommend using something that will help you keep track of where you are with the people you meet.

I am not the guy that will bug you until you tell me no or yes. You get two calls to set up a meeting. You get one meeting and then two follow-up calls to give me an answer. Past those five things, I'm on to the next person. My goal is just to have as many meetings as possible with different people. Keeping tabs on where I am with everyone helps me be more thorough.

As I sit here in late 2016, I use an app called Wunderlist, which helps me do the above.

☐ 46   BUSINESS-SHIP

"How do you keep track of conversations with connections so that you can keep up real relationships?"

If it's sales, keep good records of whom you've talked to and when. They know where you're coming from, you're not tricking anybody; they know you're trying to woo them.

If you're talking about true, honest relationships, build your reputation within your industry, draw people to you—and I've said this before—the secret is to *serve them*.

How do I keep relationships going with people I do business with? I care about them; I actually care about them. I take time to show an interest in who they are and what they do, and I truly try and be their friend. If it doesn't work out in a friendship, it's not going to work out in a business. If you can't sit down and have a beer with this person, then you probably don't want to do business with them. Do your best to be a good friend. Create a business-ship.

☐ 47   SCHOOL

At an event recently, I was asked, "Drop out of school or not?"

I found myself definitely wanting to say people should drop out of school. And I want to explain myself. Partly because I'm radical, but also partly because school, as we know it, be it public schools, colleges etc., are so geared against entrepreneurship. We're only just seeing the beginnings of universities understanding entrepreneurship generally. You often find that entrepreneurs are not good at school. And I think that's because there aren't many schools geared for the entrepreneur mindset.

Do I think you should drop out of high school to start a business? No. Do I think you should drop out of college to start a business? No. You need to be really smart to drop out of school. A degree is going to help you, that goes without saying. But they're expensive and they're not the end-all. As an entrepreneur, you will learn more in a year of running your own business than you will from getting a master's degree in business. I guarantee it.

I don't support dropping out of school in any way. I do, however, support following your passion, doing your passion, and doing work that keeps you up at night. And if school isn't doing it for you, maybe you need to take a break from it and do something that uses your skillset. During this time, do something that improves your self-esteem, and then go back to school if that's something you need. If you're in school just getting a really expensive education that you're not going to use, then drop out. But that is such a small percentage of you. Otherwise, stay in school, kids.

☐ 48   EXECUTE

"In writing a business plan, what are investors looking for—to see it from the perspective of the person or the idea?"

From my experience, a business plan is a formality. What investors are really looking for is the person's ability to execute.

Ideas are a dime a dozen. There are really good ideas out there that make no money, and there are really bad ideas out there making millions of dollars. It is not the idea, EVER. Ideas are awesome and they are great. But when it's go time, it's your ability to execute that matters.

That being said, investors want to see the bottom line. They want to see the financial projection. Everybody knows those are dreams, just big, old, fat pipe dreams but they want to see that you did your homework and in that, sometimes, investors can see whether you can execute or not.

Of course they want some return on their money and they are going to look for that in the business plan, but that's a small aspect of it. Did you write a business plan? Does it pencil? Will they make money by investing, and how much? These are four little tiny things that they check off their list, but then the other 90 percent of what they are looking for is you. Can you execute?

☐ 49 ORIGINAL CONTENT

"How do you move away from noise and towards genuine, helpful content generation without sacrificing hours of your day?"

Creating content takes time. That's why us original content guys have so many bags under our eyes. Original content is so worth it when building a brand. There are platforms out there that are geared towards trying to make it easier to create content, because that's a common struggle. Everybody wants original content, but nobody wants to spend the time to do it, so companies are trying to make that easier.

That might succeed, and I hope it does because original content is terrific, but coming from an original content creator, I am not somebody who shares content that I didn't make. You just have to carve the time out in your day, and you know what? If you get the process going, and you really nail down how to create the content, you get into the motions and you can just spit out original content.

Take time to create original content. Don't worry about the hours of time, because it's worth it. It will change the amount of your positive impact greatly.

☐ 50 ADVERTISING

"Just social media or mix in a little print?"

Unless your city has completely outlawed digital media, or if they've shut down the internet, then I would put my money on print.

Small businesses that are going for it, the build from nothing with little to no budget, my people—should spend it all on digital marketing.

Actually, I would put 100 percent of my money into Facebook posts. It's the best place to put your money, by far (in 2016). Who knows where digital marketing will be tomorrow.

☑ 51 INCUBATE

There is this place old Vegas that was dilapidated with a lot of blight. Then Tony Hsieh moved there. One of the things he started was a container park through his nonprofit. He took those shipping containers and stacked them on top of each other. He put shops inside of them. He made a stage out of them. He made restaurants out of them. He made playground out of them. He put them all in a city block and it works as a big incubator for their community where businesses come in. They grow outside of those containers and they put them outside the container park in the city to thrive and grow.

Tony knows that to have a vibrant community you need to incubate good businesses.

When I started my comedy club in downtown Salem, Oregon, I soon realized I wasn't only starting a business—I had to lift up the whole downtown community.

Are you focused solely on your business or are you also trying to improve the community around you?

☑ 52 SOCIAL MEDIA

"How do I find help with my social media campaign?"

The best way to get social media help is to find a campaign that you loved, or a business that's doing really great social media. I mean, find a company that really had ROI. Find out who did it, and then ask them to do it for you. Pay them what they want you to pay.

CEREAL

☒ 53 SMALL BUSINESS

Your small business is considered a business when you have an EIN number. "Oh well, I haven't done that yet." Well then it's not a business.

Sometimes your business is like a little baby. You love them, feed them, keep them clean and happy. Sometimes they are that monster under your bed that comes out and grabs your leg and gnaws it off. It has a life of its own—therefore it should have its own government-registered number. Just like you, you are your own entity, you are tracked by the government. So is your business.

Step one, start. Step two, get an EIN number. Your business is a monster, it's a baby, it's a wife, it's a husband, it's a pet. Treat it that way.

☐ 54 GUTS

Should you build your own dream or should you be involved in helping somebody else build their dream? That's the question. I get this question a lot and it's a simple answer. The best entrepreneurs have guts.

For instance, I have a friend who owns a few restaurants. He woke up one morning to the news that one of his restaurants was on fire. He got up, went to work, put a smile on his face, and did what he had to do. A couple of days later, he woke up to word that his other restaurant was flooded. He got up, put a smile on his face, and went to work. That is an entrepreneur.

Can you get up everyday, go to work, and take what your business is dishing out? If you'd rather get up, clock in, do work, clock out, and get on with your life, then that's perfect. We need you guys. We need a lot of you. Most of you need to do that. But if you think you've got the guts to have a business burn down and then have another business flood in the same week and still get up and put a smile on your face and go to work, then you are an entrepreneur.

☐ 55   WEBSITE

If you have enough money, hire somebody professional to do your website. You will thank your future self. Professionals are good at what they do. They know way more than you. They can build you a website for your company that will blow people away. It's just going to take a lot of money.

If you don't have money, go with something pre-made. Done is better than perfect. I will say this again and again, done is better than perfect. Hear me? Done is better than perfect. If you need a website and you don't have money, that's not an excuse to not get a website going. Get it done, get it out there. All people want to know is information. If it looks good, that's a perk. But it's got to get out there. SHIP!

☐ 56   FAKE IT

"What things about your business can you improvise, and what aspects of your business do you need to be serious about?"

Fake it until you make it. Improvising is just faking it, really. There's a theory in improv comedy: If you're blank, say something, say anything. The same thing with business. If you're blank, if you don't know where to go, or what to do—do anything. Do something. Keep taking steps forward, even if you don't know if that step is going to lead you down into the dumps or up into the glorious skies of the heaven.

If you don't know, fake it. It will happen.

☐ 57 SOMEBODY ELSE

I've made a reputation for myself as being a guy who encourages people, especially entrepreneurs, to quit their jobs and start their own company. While I'm not going back on that, I have two reasons why I think an entrepreneur should work for somebody else.

1. If you're trying to learn an industry, the bottom of a company in that industry is a great place to start.
2. If you're working in a company, on your way to the top, and that company has a buy-out option for you to become part or full owner of the company.

I just wanted to get that out here.

☐ 58 WOW

I can't tell you how important it is to wow your customer. I go into small businesses everyday. Perkbird works with small businesses. Co.W works with small businesses. I do a small business vlog. I'm in the business of small businesses. It's my life. A lot of them are terrific. They do a really great job, better than I could have ever done, but some of them are really missing that wow factor. They're just relying on discounting their product or having a cheaper, less quality product in the hopes to get more people in.

There are many chances to wow your customers in your business. They come out of the blue. Use your spidey senses. Remember their order, predict their next question and answer that, smile, or ask them how their day was.

There is a popular drive-thru coffee company here in the Northwest called Dutch Bros. They take the time to wow their customers. I don't know if it's good coffee. To tell you the truth, I think they could care less if they're coffee is the best, because they're in the business of giving you a good time and making you feel good. People would take caffeine pills if they didn't want the experience of drinking the coffee.

Wow, wow, wow. You want your customers to say, "Wow."

☐ 59   TRY HARD

There's something to be gained from failing. Here are three professional athletes: Steve Nash, Babe Ruth, Brett Favre. Steve Nash, in the year 2010 led the NBA in assists. In 1928, Babe Ruth led his baseball league in home runs; he had 54 of them. As of 2016, Brett Favre is the second most successful touchdown passer in this history of the NFL. He had 508 touchdown passes. There's only one person that has more than him and that's Peyton Manning.

Let's do some more statistics with these three guys. Steve Nash, 2010, same year he won the assist record, he was also the one that turned the ball over the most in the NBA, 259 times. In the same year that Babe Ruth hit 54 home runs, he led the league in striking out 87 times. Brett Favre, the second most successful touchdown passer, also holds the record for the most interceptions in an NFL career.

My point here is that if you're not failing, you're not trying hard enough. There's no excuse to not start your own company. The road less traveled is the one that people fail on the most, and subsequently succeed on the most. Put away that fear of failure and start your company, if you haven't already.

☐ 60 COMMUNITY

What do I think of Exclusive Networking Groups?

Let's answer this with the shit sandwich approach. Good, bad, good.

Good: Camaraderie. There are a lot of people in those groups who you know are in the game with you.

Bad: They're time consuming and cost money.

Good: They're exclusive.

I started in this arena before I could create a community around me without it being time consuming and costing money. Sales and business development are all about service and serving the community that you want to sell in. I think networking groups are a good answer, but at some point we've got to graduate from them and realize that the product or service that we're selling is good for our community, and that's why we're selling it.

I believe in being involved in your community, providing services, being a good person, being really caring about your clients, and helping them achieve their goals. As the saying goes, "If you want good friends, be a good friend."

☐ 61 KNOWING YOU

I can't stress enough on how important it is, in small business, to know what your strengths and weaknesses are. Since it's impossible to know yourself the way that other people do, we are dependent on other people's hints, clues and signs in the sky to tell us what we're good and bad at. Don't take a look at yourself and say I'm good or bad at this. LISTEN. Listen to those around you because they're going to tell you the God's honest truth about who you are.

Ask people, what do you think my strengths are? What am I good at? What am I not good at? Mostly listen because the little moments where you get an unbiased opinion about yourself are priceless. Also, consider the source, but take the general input you're getting. Listen not just to one person, not two, not three people, but the general overall consensus about what you're good at. That way when you're functioning inside your business you can get away from all the things you're not good at. You can be the person you are and not trying to be the person who you can never be.

Listen, and then that information will help you leverage your strengths to be a successful small business owner.

☐ 62   KEEP POSTING

"Which social media platform should I use in promoting my small business and how frequent should I post?"

I like this question because so many people are dealing with this right now. Go with the social media platform that you have the most traction on. That is a good starting point. Definitely have a presence in all the rest, but use the one that you have the most traction with.

As for frequency, it's all about engagement. How much engagement can you get? There really isn't a rule of thumb. It's all trial and error. Did you get some dislikes? Are people leaving your page, unfriending, or unfollowing? It's all trial and error, but trust me, it's going to be worth it in the long run if you know exactly what your tribe is looking for. Keep testing. What works one day might not work the next. You just have to keep on getting out there.

In my improv days, we used to ask: How do you become a better improv comedian? How do you become better on stage in front of people? My answer has always been this: Get on stage a lot. So what should your frequency of posts be? Post a lot! See where it goes.

☐ 63   INVESTORS

Search for investors like you would search for your phone when you lose it. You start with yourself and work your way out. Immediate family, extended family. Then you go out a little more to friends. "Hey, have you seen my phone?"

At this point if you don't have it, close family doesn't have it, your extended family doesn't have it, and your friends don't have it, you have to go to angel investors or banks. There are some professional angel investors, search for them. After that, go to a bank, but a bank is going to want something you own as collateral. Credit unions are usually the quickest to loan to small business. Also, at this point, you probably want to start looking into pitch opportunities, investing events, you know, pitch tank-type events. They're everywhere now. Go to your Chamber of Commerce. Ask them.

Search for investors like you search for your lost phone. Is it on you? Does your immediate family have it? Does your extended family have it? Do your friends have it? Then go to banks and events (not that they have ever helped me find my phone).

☒ 64   GUERILLA

Red Bull does an amazing job at creating a culture and putting their money in less obvious places to draw attention to their product. I think we can all learn from them, because we always think about marketing as print, social media, Pay per Click, or Google AdWords.

We should all challenge ourselves to put some money, attention, or time in other places, which is what guerrilla marketing is. If you don't have a lot of money to just throw at marketing, then you do have time to do something cool.

Think about ways you can do things that might attract eyeballs to your product or service that don't cost money, but costs time. Sometimes, that's all you need.

☐ 65   ENDURANCE

I've been thinking a lot about why I like to run triathlons. I'm attracted to triathlons, or any sort of race, for the same reason I'm attracted to business—it's all about endurance, and your ability to cope with mind over matter.

Endurance. It's not necessary for you to run faster than the next guy or girl. It is more important that you finish. Most people are racing to complete, not to compete. Most are in the game for the game. They like the game.

For me, the game is just enduring. The secret to success is just being the last man standing. I think that's why I like triathlons and business. Play to complete. Just put one foot in front of the other when nobody else can. That's how you win in business.

☐ 66   FIT

I can't emphasize enough how important it is to stay fit for our minds to be functioning the way they should.

Two points I want to get across today:

1. It is important to stay fit

Always work out. Schedule it into your day (I discussed this in Lesson 13 "EXERCISE"). Make sure it's something you do. Always work on getting your body better, because your brain will follow. It'll help you make better decisions.

2. Working out can get boring if there's no challenge

That's where I was. I was swimming, but then I lost interest, and then now I've found renewed life by committing to running triathlons. I want to draw out the importance of setting up a situation where working out isn't boring, such as having a goal (like my triathlons), or exercising with a friend or somebody to keep you accountable.

Make it part of your day.

☐ 67   CONSISTENCY

Being consistently okay is better than being inconsistently great.

For instance, the McDonald's empire does not have the best food. I don't even think McDonald's would say they have the best burger out there, because they don't. They have the chance to say that and they don't. But they are consistent. You know your hamburger is going to taste the same every time you go in there. It's consistently okay.

That is better than being inconsistently great. This happens a lot with small businesses and small restaurants. You have great food, everything is great, but your consistency isn't there. It could be because an efficient process hasn't been put in place for the recipes, or something as little as not being open for business when you say you will be. That's not consistent. As soon as you get a reputation for being a place with inconsistent operating hours, you're going to lose business.

Consistently okay is better than inconsistently great, but consistently great is what we're all striving for.

☐ 68   PACE

You can come across a really great idea that does well, and build a business around it and sell it, but 99.99 percent of the time it doesn't work that way. Owners say, "I'm working hard. I'm really putting in hours." Then, a couple of weeks later, they say, "Yeah, I took a weekend. I just had to repair, and I actually kind of don't want to go back to my business." Business is a marathon. It's not a sprint.

A lot of people brag on their days, "I worked 14 hours today." That's great, but how long can you keep that up? How long can people around you be able to deal with that? What are you doing with those 14 hours?

Make sure you're being efficient in the time that you are doing work, but also make sure that you're keeping a comfortable pace.

What is your pace? Can you maintain that pace?

☐ 69   RESOLUTIONS

New Year's resolutions have always bothered me because I live by the statement of "If not now, then when?" So for people to wait for a new year to make resolutions and really change their life, I feel, is a weak move.

I don't make New Year's resolutions. I wake up every morning and crush it. If I were to wait until a certain date to really start changing my life, I'd probably have a slim chance of succeeding.

Don't wait for a new year to make your resolution. Change now, change today, start today. You have what it takes to change. You just have do it and stick with it. It's all about dedication and discipline.

☐ 70   KOBE

I want everybody to turn on Jay Z's "Hard Knock Life" right now, okay? And then come back and we'll continue to roll.

Alright. Are we on the same level now?

The year is 1996. A young Kobe Bryant has just joined the Lakers. He's straight out of high school. He's already become a force, a definite leader on the team. Phil Jackson is coaching him. The season goes on. Things are going great, but Kobe starts to struggle. Phil asks him what the problem is. Kobe says that he feels like the other players are not rising to the challenge or working as hard as he is. He wants to win. He wants that Championship. He's a competitor. He's driven, he's focused, and he has goals. He's up early, he's up late, he's working before games, he's working after games, he's working before practices, and he's working after practices. He says to Phil, "I'm feeling demotivated at this point." Phil says to him, "Kobe. You're a leader. You will always be the hardest working person on your team." Kobe was letting the fact that he was the hardest working person on his team slow him down mentally.

Here's something for you leaders out there. Leaders! I'm talking to you. You will always be the hardest working person on your team. You have to get used to that. You have to be ready for that. Don't hold that against the other team members. They have their pace. They have what they're going to put on the table. Don't get upset that you're outworking everybody else. Expect it. Get ready for them. And if you see somebody outworking you, try to be as close to that person as possible. He or she will teach you some things.

☐ 71   SUCCESS

There are a lot of goals in life that pertain to working hard, giving all you've got and sacrificing everything, which will definitely pay off in the future. I wish I could say that about entrepreneurship. The really hard thing about being an entrepreneur is that the odds of you starting a company and succeeding financially are probably not that good. You might be an entrepreneur for four weeks, and you're a millionaire. You also might be an entrepreneur for 40, 50, or 60 years, and never achieve financial success.

Focus on the joy of being an entrepreneur and what it's like to work on something you love doing. I want to encourage you, just like I'm encouraging myself, that when you go through those times of financial woes, you really start to focus on the emotional success that you can already claim. You might not be very happy right now because you're broke, but be joyful because we're waking up every morning and doing something we're passionate about and are in love with. We're inspired, and we're inspiring people around us.

Financial success is uncertain, but emotional success is imminent. Let that be the payoff for you because there's no financial guarantee. That's my encouragement to you. That's my encouragement to myself.

☐ 72 CULTURE

What does your company feel like? Anybody can do what you are doing with your product or service. But can they create the culture you have established?

Take a look at what is going on in your company. What does it feel like? What's the atmosphere like? Does it feel like family? Does it feel like everybody there has got your back? Or does it feel like they want to stab you in the back? I hope that you're creating a culture that nobody else can get close to so that your company will thrive.

Culture, it gets me. I love it. I love company culture. It's such an enormous area inside every industry but I believe people are completely disregarding it.

Are you Walmart or are you Target? It's all the same stuff. How does your company feel?

☐ 73 MOVE

Einstein said, "If you stop pedaling a bike, you're going to fall over."

Always be pedaling that bike. Always be moving.

About three years ago, I developed severe neck pain. I finally ended up going to the emergency room and got an MRI. The doctor told me that I had three ruptured disks in my neck and that I was probably going to need surgery. I went to my chiropractor and said, "I want to avoid surgery. What should I do?" Should I just sit down? Lay down until this heals? "NO!" He said, "Movement is life. Movement gives you life."

That's my encouragement for you today. Always be moving. Know that in your business, movement is life. Always stay raw. Always be innovating and trying new things, because it's in those times of innovation that we really start to get our brain and our synapses on fire.

☐ 74   CORK

When you first start a company, it's just you. You're putting things together and getting money, you're doing your own marketing. Eventually, you find a partner and that partner goes on to help the company grow, and then you get a couple staff members. Then you have this huge company and everything is going great. Then all of a sudden you see it plateau.

One reason it might plateau is because sometimes we can get in the way of our own company. It's always been my philosophy that you work your way out of your company. Immediately start trying to replace yourself so eventually the company doesn't need you. What can be a pitfall, however, is when we work ourselves out of our company and stay at one final spot, and then our company stops growing. There's a bottleneck and you're the cork.

Are you being the cork in your company? Are you stopping it from growth? Work yourself out of the way. Get yourself out of the way.

☐ 75   PERKBIRD

It's all about gratitude. Just being gracious is what it's all about. If you're a follower of Gary Vaynerchuk, you've probably heard of his book, Jab, Jab, Jab, Right Hook. It's all about the jabs.

I always lead with a thank you when I'm trying to win employees, when I'm trying to win business, or when I'm trying to get people on my side. It's a good habit. It puts others in the right mood; it lets them know exactly where you're coming from and that you're not going to be that person that forgets about how important they are.

When we're trying to win clients, customers, or win employees, remember to lead with a thank you. Lead with a gift, and watch how quickly you win people over.

☐ 76   DRESS

I want to be transparent with you. I believe in the rule that you should always be the best dressed. Always dress for success. Look good, feel good, play good, do good. I live by this. Dropping the ball: I'm not the best dressed, I could do better, I really could, and that is unacceptable. There it is on the table.

Let me tell you where I'm not dropping the ball. I learned a lot of things by failing, but one of the things I got naturally was the idea that you must dress for success in your business as well. Have you ever heard of the term, dress for the job you want, like the job you want, and work for the job you want, and you will get that job? It goes along the same way with your company.

Really early on I learned that no matter how many people were in my company, be it one or 40, I always refer to my company as "us". It's very important to assume the role of a bigger company than you are at first. Be the company you want to be and eventually, you will be that company.

Is your company dressed for the type of company it wants to be? If you want to be a big company, consider yourself a "we" and not an "I".

☐ 77   MEANDER

I have this theory called the Fun Zone. I've talked about knowing what you're good at and just sticking to those three, four, or if you're gifted, five things. The other 150,000 things are somebody else's things to do. The Fun Zone is this place where you're working, you're staying within what you're good at, what gives you life. And since you're there, your output is so great. You're being so efficient. You're putting out good work. You're mass-producing a good amount of work because you're staying in the Fun Zone with the things that give you life.

Of course there are things we need to do that we don't like to do, things that don't exactly give us life, but are still in the Fun Zone (see Lesson 158 "SATURN"). I've realized that if I find myself getting down, I'm not really focused on having fun with what I do. I should be enjoying the journey. If you're always focused on, "I'm going to do this, I'm going to do that," then eventually, you will realize, "Wait a second, I haven't taken a moment to just enjoy how far I've come, and where I'm sitting right now next to these amazing people." My encouragement to you is to stay in that Fun Zone.

Remember, this is the journey that you're going through. Don't wait till you get to where you're going to celebrate. Celebrate now! Be excited now! Take a second, meander, roam around a bit where you are. Don't always just be head in the books or running somewhere, running there, being stuffy, and not having fun. Dial it up! Have a good time! Bask in the Fun Zone.

Stay in that Fun Zone. Enjoy the journey. Enjoy the people you're around and how far you've come. You've come a long ways, and I'm proud of you.

☐ 78 FOUR

I find the excuse of not having time for starting a business more and more invalid. When people say, "I'm unhappy with my job," I tell them, "Well, why don't you start a business wrapped around your passion?" Their answer? "I don't have time."

MATH TIME!

There are 24 hours in a day. The human body needs seven hours of sleep. You work eight hours at a full-time job, nine with lunch hour. 7+9 = 16. How much time do you have left? 24-16 = 8. You have eight hours in a day to start your own business.

Wait, wait, wait, Chip. I have soccer and basketball games to take the kids to. I have church. I have boy scouts. I have my bridge club. Fine! Half of those 8 hours can go to that. That's 4 hours in day, 20 hours in a week—almost a part-time job. You could be building your company, or at least starting to build your company, based on your passion.

I'm going to call it the Magic 4 Hours. You know why it's magic? It'll change your life. The Magic 4 Hours. I'm no longer taking the excuse of you not having enough time in a day to start your own company wrapped around your passion. You have four hours in each day.

Here's my challenge to you. Take those magic four and just start something. Starting? That's the hardest part. Just start. Just start something that might lead to a career inside your passion. Your family will love you more for it. Your kids will love you more for it. Your friends will love you more for it. More importantly, you will love you more for it.

☐ 79   IDEAS

People often come up to me and say, "I have this great idea and I'm thinking of starting my own business." Whether it is or isn't a good idea, I always respond, "Great! Start a company for sure." The truth is, it's not the idea that should spark the starting of a company, but your willingness and ability to execute. You should want to start a business if you have this feeling that, wow, it really charges my batteries to execute an idea.

It's not the idea. If you have a great idea, good, do it, take off and do your thing, but that shouldn't be why you want to start your own business.

You should start it because you really enjoy seeing things come together. You thrive on the achievement of having built something. You're the person that likes to stand back after they wash their car and proudly say, "Clean!" or stand back after you build a picnic table and go, "This is a picnic table." These are entrepreneurs. It has nothing to do with the idea. Really good ideas can and will fail. Really bad ideas can, will, and have succeeded.

The next time you feel like you need to start a business because you have a great idea, know that it's not the idea—your willingness and ability to execute on any idea is what should inspire you to start your own company.

☐ 80   IRONS

What do you do when you have all these things you want to do, and can't decide which one to do? Do them all. Do them all and see which one rises to the top the fastest then cut off all the rest. Fair warning, the iron and the fire process could go haywire. If you start doing them all, and one takes off but you hold on to all the rest, they could start to bog you down. And you might start doing them all terribly.

The irons that should be in the fire are the ones that are performing—that are getting red hot! If you're like me, you've learned to keep a couple in the fire. Two, three, or four. Too many, and you're not going to do anything really well. It will suck up all the heat. That's when you have to get rid of some of those irons, so that the other ones can burn bright red.

Look around you and be aware. Take a step back and see what's performing. See if one of the irons in the fire, or two, or three, or four of them are holding another one back from being super, duper hot!

☐ 81   MENTORS

I am a strong believer in mentorship, in seeking wise counsel. However, I don't have a mentor.

I have people I go to for advice when I have a big decision to make. But I believe that having a mentor is an arrangement that has more structure, where we meet every so often and are accountable. To me, mentorship involves wise counsel and accountability.

Here are two problems I have had with mentors:

1. They can't commit

Some people don't want to be mentors because it may seem like they have to take on a lot of responsibility.

2. I don't have faith in those willing to mentor me

That makes me sound terrible, but honestly, I'm not interested in a mentor who is older than me but doesn't have more experience than I do. There are a number of mentors out there who are ten years younger than me. I'd love to have them as my mentors. I just want somebody who has been through as much as I have or more.

Find somebody who can provide wise counsel and be accountable.

☐ 82   NEGATIVITY

There are many things that might deter your entrepreneurial efforts. You might be impatient, illiterate, uneducated, brash, hard to be around, not very smart (I realize that I'm describing myself), but these reasons can't prevent you from succeeding.

There is one reason that could greatly affect your success as an entrepreneur more than any others, and that is listening and keeping negative people around you. Negative people are one of the major reasons entrepreneurs do not succeed, or even start. Entrepreneurs should not listen to, surround themselves with, or let negative people be around them.

If you are hanging around negative people, or even worse, if you are listening to negative people, your chances of gaining success are diminished greatly. Negativity will bring you down quick. Don't believe the negativity. Bet on your natural abilities and get away from it.

☐ 83   SERIOUSLY

Entrepreneurs, if you ever need a boost, or proof that our society is still amazing and heading toward an amazing trajectory, go talk to some high school kids. I had the best question while speaking at a high school event:

"If you didn't go to school, how do people take you seriously?" The class laughed a little bit, and then it got awkward. I loved that awkwardness. I told my story of how I was thrown into starting my first company, but I immediately felt comfortable. I said, "I was finally in a spot where my skills were being used, then my self-esteem shot through the roof, and my confidence came through my competence. I was respected because I was finally good at something, which hadn't happened much until I then."

Why do people take you seriously? If you find that they're not, then maybe it's because you're not in a place where your natural skills are being used to their fullest potential. If they are taking you seriously, this is also a good chance to take a step back and make sure you're focused on what you're doing with life. Is your life how you set it out be?

☐ 84   MESSED-UPNESSES

There are a million great things about being an entrepreneur. You're your own boss. You're using your skills. You are accomplished. You get to do what you love to do. Sometimes, the money's good. Sometimes, it's glamorous.

People often ask me, "What is the hardest part about being an entrepreneur?"

The hardest part is seeing how my lifestyle and the decisions I've made affect those closest to me. It can be really hard to be married to an entrepreneur. It is really hard to be the son or daughter of an entrepreneur. I can see how, sometimes, my schedule, dedication, and work ethic affect the people around me negatively. The way my brain works, in all of its messed-upness that works so well with an entrepreneurial lifestyle, can also hurt those around me.

For those of you who are around and close to entrepreneurs, we're sorry. We are definitely hard to be around. And for those of you entrepreneurs, true entrepreneurs with that entrepreneurial brain, keep in mind the people around you sometimes are suffering because the really great qualities that work well in entrepreneurship don't work very well in relationships.

Entrepreneurship and relationships, they butt heads sometimes. Most of the time.

☐ 85   PRESSURE

St. Petersburg, Florida. 1989. My baseball team had one more game to make it to the championships. I was sitting the bench as usual because I was a pitcher, and a bad one at that. I had torn my rotator cuff and couldn't throw anymore, so I was useless. There were two outs, somebody on third, and the game was in the bottom of the ninth inning. It was a tie ball game.

Our number four hitter was up next. His name was Curt Thonan. He was a pitcher as well. He was huge and he threw fast, so we called him Curt "Thrownan". I was excited because now we were going to get to go to the championships because for sure Curt Thrownan was going to knock this ball out of the park. Our coach, Tim Wochdin, called a time-out and looked into the dugout. "Chip, you're batting," he says.

I immediately wet my pants. My coach meets me at home plate, and he goes, "Chip, if he strikes you out, we just go home. We lose the whole season. What we've worked for for months will be gone. That's all we have to lose. But if you get on base and we win, you're a hero."

(Side note: To this day I don't know why he took Curt out and put me in.)

I was facing Chris Masterson. Chris Masterson was about nine feet four. He had biceps bigger than my thighs, and long, flowing blonde hair. I wet my pants once more. Chris threw his fist first pitch. I didn't even see it, I just heard it—"Strike one," the umpire yelled. Here came the next ball. I missed. I look at my coach and I say, "I want out." He said, "No, go back and hit."

I step back up to the plate and close my eyes. I hear the pitch coming and I swing as hard as I can. I hit the ball right back at Chris Masterson so fast he couldn't even see it. He couldn't catch it, for sure, and it zipped into the outfield. By the time I got to the plate, my entire team was there. They lifted me above their shoulders and started screaming my name.

The lesson of this story is not that entrepreneurs perform better under pressure. The lesson of this story is that entrepreneurs only *perform* under pressure. If you're not an entrepreneur, know that about us, and change course accordingly. If you are an entrepreneur, own it. Put that pressure on yourself and don't be afraid of it. Get yourself in a situation where there is a lot of pressure. You will perform.

☐ 86 CELEBRATE

I try to be an even-keeled person. I'm not wired that way but I fight to be that way. I used to be all over the place.

Let me tell you where I am at right now. If something bad happens, I take it in stride. I try and stay even keeled. But if something good happens, I celebrate it. Depending on the magnitude of what happened, I celebrate by either getting an ice cream cone or taking a vacation, or somewhere in between.

I want to encourage you to be looking for little victories and making sure that you celebrate them. Reward yourself. What that does is perpetuate motion and help carry your steam through the rest of the journey. Hopefully you're already doing that, if not, start today. You worked hard, you sacrificed, you slaved. Celebrate your successes. You're worth it.

☐ 87   EMPLOYEE

I'm watching this series on Netflix called High Profit. It's about this couple that moved to Breckenridge, Colorado, five years before it was legal to sell marijuana recreationally. They moved there so that they could be the first ones to sell there. In the last few episodes, their employees talked down the owners because the employees felt like they weren't getting big enough raises, despite how much money they were making.

When employees see the company making money, they assume it is going into the pockets of the owner.

Employees, listen up. I'd like to make you better employees right now, with this one exercise. Here we go:

Shut your eyes. Envision your employer. The owner of the company you work for. Look at that person. Are you envisioning that person? Look into their eyes and know that that person's blood, sweat, and tears, literally, have gone into the business that you work for. That person is most likely the last to get paid. That person, for the longest time, was the least paid person in the company. Actually, at this point, that person is probably making less than you. When this person finally achieves success and gains profit in their business, don't be mad at them. They worked their ass off to get to where they currently are. They chose not to go the employee route and built a dream of their own. Sleepless nights. Unending stress. Maybe even wrecked relationships. All so that the business you work for can pay you a fair wage.

Okay. Now open your eyes. You are a better employee now. You're welcome.

☐ 88 NAPSTER

The year was 1999. The company was Napster. Napster was making a big splash in the music industry because they were allowing people to share music for free. It was spreading like wild fire. People were getting the music they want and not having to pay for it.

Two bands, Metallica and John Mayer. Two different approaches:

Metallica

They were angry. "No! That's how we make our money as musicians! We sell albums!" They did not make a lot of fans by doing that. Metallica took the approach of being very angry, very offensive, and offended that their industry evolved into a different monster.

John Mayer

John Mayer was up and coming at about this time as a singer/songwriter. He released his first album just when Napster was hitting full capacity. John Mayer said, you can have my music. I want you to get it out there. I want more people to listen to my music. He saw this as a way to get more people to fall in love with his work. He adapted to the movement in his industry. By doing that, he reconfigured how he was going to make money as a musician. He gave away what people were charging for, but charged for something else and charged more. Have you ever been to a John Mayer concert? Tickets are so expensive. He adapted. Today, everybody in the music industry makes their money from concerts and merchandise because the industry has changed.

What are you trying to charge for that other people are giving away for free? What can you leverage to get eyeballs by giving it away so that you could charge for something else?

☐ 89   SILOS

One of my buddies came to me and said that as a real estate agent, he really needs more products to offer. He feels that he needs to get out there more.

My advice to him was from my own experience in writing this book. I chose a silo within business to deal with: small business owners. You, guys and girls—starting, wanting to start, running a small business, or grew one and sold it for a billion dollars—that is who I'm my target audience is.

Here was my suggestion to my buddy: Find a place where you can give within your industry. He sells homes. I suggested he start a video log (or vlog), or start some kind of service having to do with homes, like home improvement, remodeling, or landscaping.

The best way to attract people to you is by giving them something they need. Find a silo within your industry, an area in which you constantly deal with, and give to your potential customers. Don't ask (yet).

☐ 90   SCHOOLS

This one is for high schoolers and people in college. Everybody else, stop reading. Go have some tea.

When the public school system was built, it was made to get you ready for college. College was structured to get you ready for your career, to fit you somewhere in this world of ours. I have bad news. Now more than ever, that is not happening. (I'm painting with a broad brush here, I'm sorry, but sometimes I have to.) There are some really great schools with wonderful programs, but generally, schools are not equipping people to go to college, and colleges are not equipping people for the workforce. The system is broken.

People are coming out of college ill-prepared for the working world. The worst part is, they're in a lot of debt. A lot. I don't want to be all gloom and doom, but just know that you can navigate the waters if you know the facts.

Don't leave it up to your school to get you ready for the next step. Be active. Take control of your career path. Be smart.

☐ 91 $TORY

If you sell a product or a service, raise your hand.

I have a friend who wants to put inside my co-working business. So she showed her constituents around the place in the hopes that they would support her decision. I welcomed everybody, handed it off to her and said, "All right. It's time for so and so to share her vision for this room."

This turned into an awesome moment. She started off by telling everyone a story, not by saying, "Hey. This thing is going to go here and we're going to have that thing there and this is going here." She told a story. She didn't try to sell a vision. She didn't try to sell her product or her service. She sold her story.

When people ask me to explain how Perkbird works, the very first thing I say is, "Do you have time for a story?" I don't say that Perkbird is an online-based tool that helps pair customers who are rewarded with service industry, yadda, yadda, yadda. I tell them the story of how the idea came about.

To those of you who raised your hand and said you sold a product or service, I want to challenge you. The next time you get a chance to sell your product or service, sell your story. Everybody knows about your product or service. They've heard it a thousand times, but they don't know about you, how you got there, and how you're going to take care of them. They're interested in you and your story.

☐ 92 DEMOGRAPHIC

I built a concept that could be described as a comedy club. I had the business plan all written out. I'd done my research. It all made sense. We were going to open a comedy club and then we were going to do improv comedy six nights a week, and all the 20-somethings were going to come out and have a good time and spend their money.

We started. We did an offer through Groupon. We sold 1,000 tickets in one day. 1,000 tickets in one day with Groupon! You know who bought our tickets? 45- to 60-year-old women. That's right. Do you know how many nights we did comedy after that? One night a week. There are two lessons here:

1. Start

Go ahead and start. Write your business plan. Get it going. Remember that the business plan is a living, breathing document that should be rewritten twice a year, at the very least. Rewrite that business plan because the market will tell you how to run your business. The market will tell you your demographic, what they're willing to pay for, and when they want to use your product or service. I was ready to serve comedy to 20-year-olds but came to find that it was 45- to 60-year-old women who enjoyed drinking wine and watching comedy. It still is that.

2. Listen

Your key demographic is the people who spend money at your business. Go with the data. At the same time, don't be stubborn and think, "No, no, no. I know the demographic and that's the only group I'm going to serve." Listen to your company. It'll tell you how to run it. It'll tell you where the money is. It'll tell you what your key demographic is.

Listen. Watch. Take your cues from the people who are using your product.

☐ 93   QUESTIONS

"What questions should we be asking our kids so that they can find their passion, start building their story, and be successful in life?

Here's some back-story: I don't have 14-year-old kids. However, I did go to school for youth ministries, and at my first company I dealt with a group of 14-year-old kids almost every night for about eight years, so I'd like to think that I know a little bit about the youth of today.

The important thing is that you're asking questions and getting involved. Teenagers are weird, scary monsters. Teenagers separate from everybody else and only talk amongst each other, and then they morph and find themselves. As adults, parents, and leaders in their lives, the best thing we can do is interfere every so often and say, "Hey, I'm here. I want to let you know that I love you, and I hope that is clear. I'm pursuing you but I'm also very interested in you and who you are."

I had a friend I grew up with, Corey Lopez, who is now a professional surfer. Corey Lopez started surfing the same time as I did, really early in life. He was just as good as everybody else. But then his dad started getting involved, and would take him to Costa Rica often and for weeks at a time. I'm not saying that you should take your child to Wimbledon if they like tennis, but support them if they get really into something. If they like underwater basket weaving, here's water and some wicker.

The number one thing an adult can do with a teenager is be involved in their life. Most adults aren't involved in teenagers' life and these young people just hover around. They're not being led, challenged, or asked questions. That's a big problem.

Show support in the things they are interested in. Those things will flip-flop around, but it doesn't matter. At least you gave them a chance to really excel in that one thing at that time. They might like piano, all right here's the piano, play the piano. They're eventually going to get to that one thing that sticks. If it's entrepreneurship, great! It might not be that; it might be horseback riding, or finances, or they might be really good at school.

We've got to give our youth the opportunity to bounce around on top of those gears until their gear sticks in the system. They will if they're given that opportunity. It's important that they're experiencing something they're successful with. Let them keep jumping around until they finally get into something they're good at and then support that. Then their self esteem will go through the roof.

☐ 94   BALANCE

After 20 years of being an entrepreneur and being around entrepreneurs, I've developed a highly sophisticated test that I'm almost ready to release to the public. At the end of the test, you will know if you are an entrepreneur or not.

Here's the test. Ready?

<u>Chip Conrad's Entrepreneur Test</u>

Question 1:

Jump

Did you jump? If you said no, you're not an entrepreneur.

If you jumped out some window or a car, without asking questions and without really analyzing what a jump is, if you didn't ask why, then you are an entrepreneur.

END OF TEST

Pretty sophisticated, isn't it? I'm taking the long way to tell you that if you have to ask if entrepreneurship is for you then stay with the J-O-B. That's almost everybody out there. Don't feel like you're the minority. How do you balance? There is no balance. There is, "You do, or you don't", "You live or you die", "You fail or you succeed." That's the risk entrepreneur's take.

There's no guarantee in being an entrepreneur. There is a guarantee being in a job—you worked hours, you get paid. You get a paycheck, there is a signature on it, and that signature is usually of an entrepreneur.

☐ 95   MOMENTUM

"How do we deal with success?"

Celebrate. Go out and say, "We did it. We won," but not for too long. The momentum might pass you by.

Momentum feels a lot like surfing. When you surf, you sit in the water until a wave comes. You push the board with your arms until eventually, the wave takes over and you are caught right in the momentum of the wave. Your momentum and the wave's momentum catch up to each other. The wave pushes you, but you get to stay in the sweet spot or else the wave will pass you by, or you'll get too much in front of it and crash.

If you celebrate too long, you pull out in front of it the wave and it crashes on you. If you don't celebrate at all—maybe you're too focused on day-to-day, not really liking it, and not really paying attention to the momentum—then the momentum will pass you by. Ride that momentum. Make sure you're in the right place.

Keep yourself at the place where you do the best work, where you do the most. Ride the momentum.

☐ 96 PASSION

When I meet with clients, one of the first questions I ask them is, "Do you have a passion for what you're doing?"

Here's why I ask. If your passion is just money, we're probably not going to mix well. Secondly, if you don't live, eat, sleep, and breathe what you're doing—if you really don't dig on it—I won't work with you, because it's that passion that drives us.

So, do you have a passion for what you're doing? To those of you who are working a J-O-B and moonlighting to grow a business that will take over that J-O-B, do you absolutely love it or are you in the love with the idea of it? There's big difference.

Don't just have a passion for the start. Have a passion for the industry you are in, so that you can finish and finish strong.

☐ 97   BUSKING

The year: 2002 (or 2003). The group: Isaac Improv. We were on our first tour in California. I was very young, driven, and ambitious (like now, only not as young). We had a show that night in one of the Bay Area suburbs. We arrived early because I had an awesome idea: We would go to the main strip by the wharf in the city of San Francisco and busk for the first time. We weren't going to ask for money; we were just going to perform and invite people to our show that night. It didn't exactly work out like I wanted it to because I didn't have the buy-in from the whole team. So we didn't get to do it. This reminds me of people's approach to marketing.

So many people think that social media is "The Show". It's not. The show is where you have contacts to potential clients or customers—emails, addresses, phone numbers. Do you have your own business page on Facebook? Here's a surprise: It's not your page, it's Facebook's. Everything on Facebook belongs to Facebook. Everything on social media is not yours. Social media is just the busking part. It's where you go to perform and invite people to your show.

Make sure you're only using social media to busk. Realize that social media is not where you own your tribe. Your splash page or web page, where you collect people's information, that's the show. That's the focus. Social media is just to drive people to that focus.

☐ 98   LOYALTY

We have a Kegerator at our co-working space (because we are in the Northwest and you can't run a business without serving microbrew). We had some problems with it: It was using up carbon dioxide too quickly. After going through three bottles of CO_2 in a month, I called for help. His name is Jared. He showed up and I told him, "You take over. I'm done with it." He says, "No problem."

I saw him tinker around. He goes all the way back down to his car. He comes back up with a tank.

"It's all fixed."

"Perfect, thank you so much. You've been such a help. What is the damage?"

"No damage at all. No fee for the day. First one's on me." He shakes my hand and leaves.

Jared knew that creating loyal customers is sometimes worth more than the fee you charge. I'm not saying to only create loyalty and not charge people. I'm saying that you should test the waters. Listen, see, and sense the situation. If you think that creating a loyal customer is worth way more than the money you're about to charge, then don't charge them. Again, I'm not saying to walk around not charging people for your service. As a matter of fact, I usually say the opposite—make sure you charge a premium for your service because your service is premium.

Sometimes creating a loyal customer is worth way more than charging that customer your fee. It doesn't happen often, but search for that moment because what Jared did made me want to recommend him to people who might need his service.

☐ 99   DICK

The year: 2007. The place: San Diego, California. The company: State Farm. I hate to admit it, but I once tried to get outside the warm and comfy confines of the risky landscape that is entrepreneurship, and I was an employee of an insurance agency. I had just sold my surfboard manufacturing company and didn't know what to do, so I got a job selling insurance.

I was slinging insurance and doing a really good job. My boss was a guy named Dick. Dick was old, crotchety, terrible to be around, but I loved him. He was insanely bright. He had so much experience. I knew this job was going to suck, but I knew I could learn some good habits from Dick.

One day he came up to me and he said, "Chip, it is important after every time you make a sale, the last thing you say to your new client is, "You've made an amazing decision. You're going to be happy with us."" From that day on, anytime I closed a sale, deal, or contract, the last thing I say is something to the effect of, "You have made an amazing decision." I say it because:

1. It's true.
2. What is the first thing that happens to somebody when they buy something? They immediately think, "I wonder if I made a good decision or not?" If you beat them to the punch and let them know that they did make a good decision, you set that relationship off in the right direction from the very start.

On your next sale, after your client says, "Yes I want it," make sure you respond with, "You've made an amazing decision." See how that changes your relationship with them.

☐ 100   PREDICTABLE

Small business is great. They are not governed by hot-shot corporate suits that procedure-ize every little aspect of the company.

The bad part is that the lack of structure leads to highly unpredictable business habits. Have you ever gone to your favorite shop and the sign on the door read: "Off to _____. Be back soon." Or have you ever gone to your favorite taco joint and the tacos don't taste like the last time you were there? This is because the right procedures have not been put in place. McDonald's doesn't have the best burger in town. They just have the most predictable burger.

You're small and that's great. Make sure you take the time to get it right every time. Be good, but also be predictable.

☐ 101   BUY-IN

Getting your team to buy-in to your company is challenging. Every owner wants their employees to be as jazzed as they are about the business. It all starts with the mission statement. I'm always surprised to learn that many companies don't have one. Mission statements ensure that every employee knows what the business is all about. If an outsider asks for the mission statement of your company, any employee should be able to recite it. Not everybody's going to have the buy-in, and that's not an employee's job, unless that's your company's culture. Zappo's has a culture guide that is written every year by its employees. It's a book written by the employees, telling new employees how the company functions.

For example: Our mission is to make good cupcakes. If that's not what you want to do here, then maybe you're not a good fit.

☐ 102 BE OUTSTANDING

The year: 1994. I was living in St. Pete, Florida. I wanted a job at a major electronic store. At the time, my dad was the VP of this company. I could have called him, he could have made a call, and I would have had a job. I didn't want to do that. I wanted to get the job on my own scruples.

I went in. I applied. I got the job. After working at this location for a few months I started to realize why they were not performing well and I left as soon as I could.

I eventually let my dad know that I had gotten a job at his company but left. After he asked why I explained to him a few of the things (bad things) that were going on there. A few months after that, I visited the store to buy something. The staff and the feel of the store had drastically changed.

I'm not saying those changes were directly because of my conversation with my dad, but I want to bring to light the point that you never know whom you're talking to in your business, whether it be a customer or employee. We are all connected and that connection might lead to someone who is very influential. You might as well be yourself. Be outstanding. You might as well be a genuine, gracious, positive, and selfless person.

Because you might be dealing with your boss's boss's boss's son.

☐ 103   VALUES

What are your core values? I came up with three: Love, Family, Passion. My biggest goal is to try and build a personal filter that causes me to ask myself three questions before I do anything:

1. Am I doing this out of love or hate? Am I being caring or not? Am I being reckless or not? Is this out of love?
2. Is what I'm doing going to be good for the family?
3. Am I doing this inside my passion or am I going outside of my passion?

What are your three core values?

☐ 104   LINE

I was having lunch with one of my buddies who sells real estate in Salem. He brought up an interesting point about the fact that he only works Monday through Thursday. He told me that the effect was having the opposite of what he thought might happen—that it was drawing more attention to him.

Here's why I think that is. I had a comedy club in St. Pete, Florida, and attendance was low. So we started opening the doors a half an hour after we said we would. A line formed outside the comedy club, and the people driving past would see that there was a line, thus drawing them in.

We can get busy and think that it's bad because we can't get to the people we want to get to. But if a line is forming for you, chances are that it's going to draw more people to you. I'm not saying to create a fake line like we did at the comedy club. I'm saying that we should slow down, schedule another meeting next week instead of trying to fit it in this week. It's okay if a line is forming for you. It does nothing but form a larger line.

☐ 105 BREATHE

Hard work is what it takes. It's not a lucky bat, it's not a lucky hat, it's hard work. The lucky bat and the lucky hat, those help, I'm not going to lie. Most of the successes that I've had have been luck, but just like Jon Bon Jovi says, "It's like the harder I work, the luckier I get." Let's talk about that hard work. It comes in lots of different forms. The most popular form is wake up early, stay up late. Work. Meeting. Run. Repeat.

There's a different kind of hard work called patience. "Patience" is a strong word, or at least a tough one. Serial entrepreneurs have a lot on their list but sometimes that list can run a little dry. Sometimes you have to sit back and wait. It sounds funny, but hard work is also being patient.

I've been around a lot of songwriters in my life, and I've written a couple songs with my band Chip Conrad and the Concrete Feat (Google it). One of the most important things songwriters say is that sometimes, you just have to let it breathe.

Let's all take a look at where we are and not freak out when our schedule lets us take a breath. Sometimes you have to let things simmer. Boil off the water so that the true flavor can come out of our product.

☐ 106   IGNITION

This lesson is for those of you who are thinking about starting a business.

So many people look at competition as a bad thing. Most really successful entrepreneurs are not motivated by money. Sometimes, they are motivated by the game. Actually, most of the time it's the game. Last week a person came up to my co-working space and told us, "I just want to be frank with you. I'm opening up a co-working space in Salem as well." I have to say, that did nothing but ignite my drive even more. I love it.

The story of the Wright Brothers and the race with their competitors in a perfect example. The greatest companies of today would not be so great without competition. That's largely why we're in it. It's a game. Bring it on. Bring on the competition. You're only going to make each other better.

☐ 107   GUT

I've jumped off projects. I've stayed on projects for way too long. I've stayed in companies way too long. I've given up on companies way too early. I've stayed in just the right time.

When it comes to deciding whether to stay or leave a project, you have to go with your gut feeling. That's the risky part about being an entrepreneur. You just don't know.

As an entrepreneur, you start a company and from that point on you just don't know. I've seen companies that I thought had no chance of success but then, boom, they works. I've also seen companies that have the greatest people in the world but aren't successful at all.

Go with your gut.

☐ 108   FINISH

Are you getting bogged down? Maybe you're getting too far ahead of yourself. Maybe you have your head so far in that you're forgetting the big picture. A big picture example, for me, was when I committed to make video blogs every day of the week with entrepreneurial advice. There were people who depended on it. As much as I didn't feel like it some days, I kept doing it because I knew that once I downloaded the footage and started editing, I'd be really glad that I followed through.

Be encouraged, if you're feeling bogged down. There's no secret to victory—just follow through with what you said you were going to do. Just push forward.

☐ 109   FIT

Around winter of 2012, I was on a layover in Denver when my neck started hurting intensely. It had been hurting for a couple days before that, but boy, was it bad when I got to Denver. I managed to make it through another flight to Florida, but when I got there I spent the next week in a doctor's office trying to figure out what was wrong. Eventually they found that I had three ruptured discs in my neck and said I was going to need surgery. It would be a very risky surgery. They'd have to cut right next to my jugular then they would put discs in my spine right through the front of my neck. They said there was a 50/50 chance the surgery could make it worse. Those were odds I didn't like. I asked if there were any other options for me. They told me I could try and rehabilitation, build up those muscles in my neck, but that likely wouldn't help.

I started rehab when I returned to Oregon. The doctor prescribed swimming. Long story long, I started swimming four years ago. The change that physical fitness has brought to my life is extensive. I started swimming to fix my neck, but what it did was fix my professional life as well. Staying fit, being active, and keeping on the move will improve every area of your life. Get fit. Get better.

☐ 110   IGNORANCE

I moved to Salem, Oregon in 2009 and decided that I wanted to open a comedy club. This was at a time when the core of downtown Salem would shut down at 9 or 10 p.m.. Many people told me that this would never work. They said that Salem wouldn't be interested in it, Salem is a lame town, people don't go out after 9, and that they're definitely not interested in something as adventurous as live comedy. I didn't believe them and decided to move forward in my ignorance.

For the most part they were right, but I decided to focus on building a community around me and latching on to people that were doing the same thing around our downtown core. I realized that the better the community did, the better my business would do. This lead to massive success for the comedy club. If I had added up all the numbers and tested the market, the evidence would show that there was no way Salem would support a comedy club.

Two takeaways from this experience:

1. **Sometimes ignorance is the best thing for us as entrepreneurs**

We just don't know how dangerous it is.

2. **Sometimes your market analysis could turn out to be absolutely wrong**

We can turn ourselves off from something we want to do because the numbers are off. Testing the market, proof of concept, those are all important, but sometimes they are not always indicative of the potential success of a business.

☐ 111 TRANSPARENCY

One thing I stick to being is transparent. Being transparent is key to success in your personal branding. Letting people see the real you will show them what they're getting. They'll be able to decide whether or not they're getting what they're looking for.

To those who have a personal brand, I encourage you to be transparent. Make a little tweak to your personal brand and see if that changes your effectiveness and ability to attract people to you.

☐ 112 HARD

I can't tell you how many times I daydream about getting a job. I talk to a lot of entrepreneurs about this. It's akin to a smoker who quit, but still yearns to have a cigarette when something tough happens. As an entrepreneur, when times get tough, the first thing we think about is, man, I could just go get a job at Home Depot. I could go work for somebody and just clock in–clock out, collect my salary and benefits, and then leave work.

What a relief that lifestyle would be for some entrepreneurs. That's not to take anything away those who have jobs, I know a lot of really hard workers with jobs. All I'm saying is, when entrepreneurs feel like giving up, they daydream about getting a job. That's how hard it is to be an entrepreneur. You're sacrificing across the board. Everything. Personal and professional.

If you want to be an entrepreneur, get ready for it to be really hard. If you're getting ready to start a business and you're mulling it over, know that it is going to be the hardest thing you've done. Ever. (Except for parenting.)

☐ 113   TEAM

Team. There is an "I" in it, and it's you. So if there is an "I" and "U" in it…it's spelled TEIAUM.

The year was 1999, and we set off on the first tour of our improv comedy troupe on the Eastern seaboard. I made a decision early on that I was going to put myself last at any occasion that I could. My job was to serve the company and my team. When we stayed at hotels or people's houses, we couldn't afford multiple rooms. I would always take the floor. I did my best to put everybody above me, until they started putting me above them.

One of the first things I do when I'm building a team is put myself last. I make it clear that I'm here to serve and help them do what they need to do on that team. They are greater than I am; I am last. Make yourself last. Eventually, you'll gain their respect. Once you've earned their respect, you'll stop sleeping on the floor, figuratively and literally.

☐ 114   HIRE

The time is never right to hire your first employee. The time is often right to hire your first three, four, or five employees. Here's why you don't want to hire one person for your first employee: Once you transition from a business without employees to one with employees, you're opening yourself up to a lot of liability, and with that comes insurance, other taxes, payroll, and all the muck that comes with that.

Hiring one person? Not really worth it because you have to pay them about $20 or $25 an hour, and everything else that costs is going to add about another $5 or $10 on top of that. However, if you hire three people, it's not another $5 or $10 per person, it's just $5 or $10 dollars overall now that you've started hiring people.

If you do feel the need, go through a temp agency. Hire somebody on contract.

☐ 115   FIRE

I think it's time to leave a client when the majority of the work is mentally dealing with that client. In a good situation, you can do what you do and they get to do what they do. Of course, clients aren't always going to agree. But when the client is being so impossible, threatening, and counterproductive that the majority of the work is you dealing with them, then it's time to let go. I have a few friends who run a brewery, and they have one rule in dealing with clients—if you can't sit down and have a drink with them, then they're not doing business with you.

Set standards before you start attracting customers. Or, if you're already attracting customers, stop and set standards for what you're looking for in a future customer or a client. That way you're going to stop some of the bad customers from getting through, although you're not going to stop all of them. We're always going to have bad customers. We're always going to have to fire clients. We're always going to have to turn down jobs. But if we set our standards and we know what we're looking for in a customer before we go out looking, that will minimize damage in the future. As for firing a customer, the same rule as firing anybody applies: Fire super fast. Hire super slow.

☐ 116   TIME

Time management:

1. **You need to have realistic expectations**

   There are only 24 hours in the day. Don't plan for 25.

2. **You need a lot less sleep than you think**

   If you work eight hours a day and you spend four hours a day with your family, you still have four hours to do work and eight hours to sleep (see Lesson 78 "FOUR"). Did I just blow your mind? That is a ton of hours. If you haven't already, use them to start your own company and create jobs in your community.

3. **Structure, structure, structure**

   Have every hour of your day planned out, even the fun and exercise should be in the plan. Have a schedule for everything. I have a schedule for how quickly it takes me to get from my daughter's school to my office. I have a schedule of how many hours I'm going to work on that specific company during the day. I have a special time to reward myself. I have a special time for fitness. I book that in as a meeting so nobody can book on top of it.

What often happens is that we end up drifting. We didn't do something during the time allotted. Your block shouldn't be, "Go to work from 8 to 5." Your block should be, "Work this issue from 8 to 9. Next issue from 9 to 10. Break. 10 to 10:15. 10 to 10:30…"

Have structure for time management then watch your output shoot through the roof.

☐ 117 GET TESTED

If you've bought this book, it's likely that you are starting or have started your own business. It's important to know yourself as an entrepreneur. Part of knowing yourself is getting tested for ADHD. A large percentage of entrepreneurs have ADHD, so it is important to deal with this subject on a book about entrepreneurship.

I'm somebody who has been clinically diagnosed with ADHD. I have spent a lot of time studying and developing systems for it.

Lets do a quick check: Do people around you say you might have ADHD? Do you often have trouble sleeping? Do you find it hard to focus on something for a long period of time? Do you suffer from anxiety or dyslexia? If you've answered yes to most of these questions, go get checked. It's better to know before you go.

Get tested. If you do not have ADHD, then thank your lucky stars. If you do, then you need to develop systems, or take medication to help you navigate through life with Attention Deficit Hyperactivity Disorder.

☐ 118   DIVERSALIZE

Make sure you diversalize. Diversify inside your specialization.

Inside your company are parameters, in accordance with your mission statement. Don't get outside of those parameters or mission statement. When you get an LLC, they make you say what your company does, because that company does what it does. Don't have an identity crisis. Don't cause people to say, "What in the world does your company do? I saw it doing this and now it's doing something else. It seems wishy-washy." If you have a business but you're looking to do something outside of it, make them two separate businesses.

In 2002, I grew my improv comedy troupe to a full-on business where we were on the road 24/7 doing 250 shows a year. About 5 years in, I started getting a little antsy. Somebody approached me and said, "Wait a second. You're performing. You're managing. You're booking and handling the operations of your company. Would you like to do that for our company?" And so we started a booking agency. That seems like a different company but it isn't. It was inside the mission of company. We were a touring improv comedy troupe that also booked other groups. I was staying specialized in what I do. I was diversifying within my company.

Stick within your mission statement. You'll save a lot of time, heartache, and moolah.

☐ 119 YOUTHS

Last week, I got a chance to interview several high school kids. I told each of them I'm an entrepreneur and asked them if they knew what that was. Most of them didn't. When I asked if they realized that they could start their own company and build it from the ground up, it seemed like it was the first time anybody had said that to the majority of these kids. To me, that was a scary moment.

I encourage you to take the time to sit down with young people, if you are around them regularly, and let them know that they have the opportunity to be an entrepreneur. They have the right to build a company from the ground up by themselves and fulfill their dreams of working within their passion, by starting their own company.

When I think about it, I was an entrepreneur before I knew what an entrepreneur was. I mowed lawns. I started my own printed t-shirt company. Then I started Isaac Improv, which was my first legitimate entity. Then I learned I had the opportunity to do that all along.

☐ 120 FILTER

As a small business owner, it is so important not only to surround yourself with positive people, but to be a positive person yourself. Take note of what you are saying and how much of that is positive and/or negative.

Let's all be more aware of what we're putting out there into the world, be it social media or talking to friends. Build a filter in your mind that asks whether or not what you're saying and doing is positive.

☐ 121   PITCH

My buddy asked me what I thought about his sales pitch. He was prepping for a meeting. I knew whom he was meeting with very well and I told him, "The way you're going to win this pitch is if you just be you."

People don't want to be sold any more. Not that they ever really did, but now especially not. The elevator pitch has taken over. These days, you have to be able to describe your product or service very quickly. More importantly, customers want you to have a relationship with them. They want to know about you. They want to know that you like dogs, that you like surfing. Mostly, they want to know that you care, and that you're not just trying to get them to buy something. The way to do that is to have that relationship. Your product or service deserves more respect than just the pitch.

Develop your pitch. Have a very short statement that describes what your product or service is. That's a definite. At the same time, throw away your sales pitch attitude, and just be you. Connect with the people you're selling your service or product to on a personal level. Tell your story.

☐ 122   OBJECTION

In sales if you have an objection, it's over. You've already lost. The objection is the end. The customer's "No" is the end. Move on.

Try not to get to the "No". The idea is to have that relationship in such a way that you never get to a "No" or an objection. It might get to a question, which is just a matter of getting them to understand why your service or product is so good for them.

☐ 123   WORRY

As entrepreneurs, we have a tendency to worry about a lot of things in our business, such as staff, revenue, getting sued, neighbors, and landlords—there are all kinds of things we can worry about. Today, I want to talk about worrying about your customers, how to do it, and at what capacity you operate with your customer.

Customers have a tendency to tell you what they want from your business. Not necessarily how to run it, but they can tell you what you need. For instance, you might worry about making the right cupcakes. "We make cupcakes so we need to have green cupcakes. Guys, hurry up. We need green cupcakes." You might never sell a green cupcake, yet you spent all this time worrying about where you're going to get the dye, what's the recipe, and how many you're going to make.

Don't worry about something inside your company until it is something to worry about; until your customers have made it known that it is something you should worry about. You might be building something, worrying about something, or losing sleep over something that your customers are never going to ask for.

☐ 124 INFRASTRUCTURE

If you have an idea for a business, start doing the business. Put the receipts for what you're spending in a shoe box. Run the business. Run income through you, and taxes if needed. When you start growing, you will find that you will have need for infrastructure and the protection of your personal assets. That is when you should start setting up your infrastructure.

Don't start the infrastructure first. You want to start a coffee shop? Start looking at coffee. Start looking at suppliers. Start looking at what you want in the shop, and eventually somebody's going to say, "Hey, when you sign this lease, do you want your company's name to be on it?" Well, then you go start a company. It takes a day.

Your company is not your relationship with the state or the federal government. Your company is you, and the things that you do in it. Do work. Start today. Build the entire infrastructure, legal contracts, etc. after you start going, when you need them. Start first. Start today.

☐ 125   FEAR

My wife and I have two children. When they were six and three years old, they would frequently come into our bed at night. Most of the time, it was because they were afraid of something. I remember doing the same thing with my parents. Fear is so real.

People talk to me a lot about starting their own business. They have their idea and plan all figured out. When I ask them why they're not going to pull the trigger, they say, "I'm just so afraid." Most entrepreneurs don't have fear as much as they have ignorance. Ignorance is one of our greatest characteristics. It's ignorance that keeps us from going, "Oh wait this is risky AF."

To those of you feeling fearful, take a second thought about entrepreneurship. Ask yourself if you truly want to be an entrepreneur, knowing that usually, entrepreneurs don't have much fear when it comes to starting a company. The day after, when it's already too late, is when we worry and feel the pressure.

If you have that fear and you want to push through, trust me, I know how fear can just stop you. Go to your parents' proverbial bed and bask in the warmth of their bosom and start that company.

☐ 126   TEACH

There is a BBQ restaurant in San Diego that I used to frequent. The best BBQ I've ever tasted. They have amazing food but they are also an amazing company. Here's something cool about them:

You know that time between Thanksgiving and New Year's? They shut down their business temporarily. They don't stop paying their employees. They just close down. Everybody takes a vacation.

I bring this up to prove a point—teach your customers how to treat you. That goes from being predictable, like being open when you say you're going to be open, to how you'll treat them as customers. At this BBQ restaurant, for example, they're telling their customers, "There are some basic things you need to know before you become my customer. We're going to be closed from Thanksgiving to New Year's."

Don't let your customers take the higher status with you. You're there to serve them but that doesn't mean that you let them walk all over you. Set your parameters. Teach them how to treat you. If they're not going to treat you how you want to be treated, then they don't deserve to be your customers.

☐ 127   GOALS

My first goal was to travel the world and make a living running my own company. By age 26, I had achieved them. I found myself searching for the next goal. For a long time, I floundered. I think it was because I didn't think I was going to achieve my first goal so early.

People often tell you, "Make sure your goals are achievable." I'm actually going to push back on that because I don't think that that's true.

Make sure that you set your goals to be mostly *un*attainable. If you set low-hanging, achievable goals, you'll likely achieve those goals, and then what are you going to do? Set goals way out in front of you. Blue-sky goals so that when you achieve them, it's probably time for you to retire.

My new one? World domination.

☐ 128   GREYISH

As you know, I don't like working with clients whom I wouldn't hang out with anyways. If I can't have a beer, throw horse shoes, or go fishing with you, then I probably don't want to work with you. On the flip side, if I want to work with you, I'm probably not going to give up trying to work with you.

We can phone it in, but how much better would it be if we really cared about that client, if we really would like to hang out with them? As you approach clients or deal with customers, try to make an effort to show that you care about them, and see if it changes the feel of work between you and your client.

If you don't care about that person but they want to do business with you, maybe you shouldn't do business with them. Say no.

☐ 129   R.F.B.

What is it about the human brain that tries to overlook red flags? This has probably happened to you: You meet a hot and popular girl or guy in high school, you get to know them, and then little things start to pop up. A little red flag—they have dirt under their nails every time you see them. Or you're way older or younger than them. Or they smell different. Not bad, just different. Something in our brain makes us go right past those early warning signs. Later on, you get into a relationship and all these red flags come back up and become the thing you can't stand about that person. Why are we so red flag-blinded?

This happens to us in business too. We have a client or a job we really want. We start dealing with them. We get in the proverbial bed with them, and as we're getting to know this person, a little red flag pops up. He just lied. He didn't sign the contract. He will. He won't lie to me. This person has a really bad reputation, but he won't burn me. He's burned everybody else. We get red flag-blindness. We start doing business with this person and all of a sudden…Red flags everywhere. Then inevitably we get hosed.

Lets all not have red flag-blindness. The next time you really want that client or customer, or you really want to start working with that freelancer, and a red flag comes up, let's end it right there. I think we will be a lot better off for it.

☐ 130   PUNCTUAL

I got a text from a close friend and colleague: "I'm at your office. I'm only waiting five minutes." I frrreaked. I thought I was late to a meeting. I freaked out because I happen to be very punctual.

When you are late to a meeting, and you have not announced or declared that you may be late, even one minute after the start of that meeting, what you're saying is, "This time is not important to me." That's why I freaked out, because your time is important to me. You are important to me. I will not be late to your meeting, and if I am, I'm going to tell you early and often. I will not show up to your meeting late.

I have let some people down. Things fall behind schedules, technology fails you, miscommunication, etc…but if you and I set a meeting, I will not be late to your meeting because I care about you.

☐ 131   MINIMUN WAGE

I was asked what I thought about the minimum wage hike in my home state of Oregon.

On one hand, if you don't help everybody go up, then we start to polarize as a country. On the other hand, as business owners, we work so hard, and then we get hit with self-employment tax and all other kinds of taxes. Higher wages for employees is another cost to worry about.

I fall right in the middle. I don't want our state/country to be polarized, but at the same time, I'd like to make minimum wage. That would be awesome.

To be honest I care very little. Lets say that business is a football game and the government is the referee. I hear coaches say it all the time. *Play the game so well that even if the referees make bad calls against you, you still beat your opponent.* That's what I think.

☐ 132 POLITICS

I was talking to a reporter from The Statesman Journal, Salem's local news rag. He started getting into politics. Politics are great. If you like politics, that's cool. No diss on you. No diss on politics. I'm just not very political, but he started talking about politics and how it affects my business. I drew a comparison, and I'll draw it for you right now as well:

When you open up a business, you should expect things to happen to you that you have no control over. Somebody could sue you for some reason you never could have ever imagined. As a business owner, you have to be prepared for the unexpected. For me, the government's dealings in my business fall into that category of the "unexpected".

That's why I don't get too political. I bunch it all together. Politics, me getting sued, my industry going kaput, or China figuring out how to do what I do a lot better, quicker and cheaper than I can …They're all grouped into the same category. It's imminent. These things are going to happen. Just be ready for them, to do them, and move on. Your job is to run a business that eventually makes money, and you take a tiny piece of it, and give the rest of it to your employees and to the government. If that's not what you like, then don't run a business.

Being an entrepreneur is like making a pie for yourself, and right when you get ready to eat it, you have to give it to everybody else, and do that every day for five years before you get your first bite.

So vote! Let your voice be heard. Then get back to work. Time is a-wasting.

☐ 133   THE LINE

When you're selling things, you have to reach out to people. Some of the time, people don't know that they need your service or product so you have to go out and let them know that. That's called marketing. Inside marketing we have this thing called sales. Sales is a more aggressive way to have somebody buy your product or service. I am often making phone calls, talking to people, reaching out, and trying to convince them of the right thing, which is that they need the service or product that I provide. There's something I often say to people I'm reaching out to, along the lines of, "Hey Susie, just following up with you, trying to ride the line between persistent and annoying, hopefully that's working, give me a call back when you can."

Here's what that does:

1. You're being open and honest
2. It lets them know that you care about how you're coming across to them, and how much you are bothering them. I do not want to be annoying.

I ride that line between persistent and annoying. I definitely want to be seen as persistent but I also don't want to be seen as annoying. I want to stay right in the middle. If you're not having somebody tell you you're slightly annoying, then you're not really riding that line. If you're not having people tell you you're slightly persistent, you're not riding that line. You want to get right in between, in that sweet spot.

☐ 134 HASTE

One day while driving my kids to school, I witnessed a situation that could have ended badly. I was in the turn lane and we were waiting for traffic so we could turn left. That's when I noticed, out of the corner of my eye, a gentleman who looked like he was going to cross the street in the middle of all of this. I looked at him, he looked at me, and sure enough, he took off. Cars slammed on the brakes, everybody hit their horns, he dashed across the street, but he made it. I was glad I did not see somebody die.

At that point, from the backseat of my car, I hear a little, tiny voice.

"Dad, that guy is not very smart, is he?"

"That guy just made a decision that was very not smart, but I don't know if he is smart or not. What I do know is that haste makes waste." Then I spent the next ten minutes explaining to her what that means.

Haste does make waste, when you're getting ready to go on a trip, when you're typing a report, grocery shopping, planting a garden, babysitting a gerbil, hand-gliding with a marsupial, having tea with a pterodactyl.

Haste doesn't make waste all the time in business. As a matter of fact, we are living in the golden age, the day where moving fast and having haste does not necessarily make waste. I would like to encourage you to innovate quickly and move fast. Try and break things. Throw caution to the wind. Let her rip. Point, shoot, aim. See what happens. In the day and age of technology, we can move so fast. Don't turn your back on haste.

☐ 135 HELP WANTED

As entrepreneurs, it is hard for us to go past a "Help Wanted" sign and not think, "I could get that job. I would knock it out of the park. I'd be making double what I'm making now." We dream about clocking in, doing the job, clocking out and never thinking about it for a good sixteen hours. It would be awesome to not have this constant, nagging pressure of decisions and relationships hanging over our heads. But alas, it is our allergy to bosses that keeps us away from that situation. Then, reality sets in and we remember—we're playing the long game. We have a plan infused with joy and passion (not always happiness) in doing what we love to do. It's actually making a living for us.

Think of your job as something you can clock out of. There needs to be some time during the day where you actually do clock out. Compartmentalize your life. Tell yourself, "I'm not going to think about being an entrepreneur for the next four hours. All I'm going to think about is being a dad or a wife or a husband or a daughter or a son or a surfer or a bicyclist or a runner or a gerbil babysitter."

It's those clocked-out times that will help our ideas come flowing through.

☐ 136   LAUNDRY

My wife used to do my laundry for me. About three years ago, we moved into a new house and I started noticing that my clothes were shrinking. Eventually after three or four shirts of mine shrunk, I said, "Babe, just let me do my laundry and you can do yours." She agreed to the new plan. A few months later, I realized that I was shrinking a lot of shirts too. I couldn't figure out why. One day, our son's toy fell behind the washer and dryer. When I went to get it, I noticed that the hoses to the washer were crossed. The red hose was going to the cold nozzle and the blue hose was going to the hot nozzle. I realized that it was I who had installed the washer and dryer. It was I who messed up the connections. So it was I who was ruining all the shirts. I was the very root of the problem.

Have you checked to make sure that you are not the root cause for the issues faced in your small business? Is it you and your systems? Is it any of your weaknesses? Is it you putting people in the wrong spot?

If you're having issues, first check to make sure it's not you. You might save a lot of time.

☐ 137   FUN

As entrepreneurs, we try and do it all then we get too bogged down with things we don't like doing. For some, it's dealing with finances, or customers, or building something with your hands when you're not a builder. We're too afraid to enlist help.

While it's true that entrepreneurs need to be mavericks, we should not get bogged down by things that we hate doing. We won't do them well, and in the long term, you'll end up wasting more money.

Let's flip that to positive: In the long run, you'll end up making money by staying in your Fun Zone and hiring out the things you don't like to do. It's more affordable than you think.

☐ 138 FUNNEL

If you have a personal brand, the goal is to sell your product with your personal brand, be it through social media, community involvement, advertising, or networking. What you're trying to do is help others realize that they need the product or service that you offer. It can look like a funnel.

You can have lots of funnels, but pay attention to the funnels you have. Make sure they're all channeling to one thing. For example: Your social media bios should have a link that leads to your webpage or the page that has the thing you sell. Your email signature should have a link to the page that has the thing you sell. You voice mail should say what it is you sell.

What's the one thing you're selling, and do all of your funnels lead to it? Or do you have funnels going the wrong way? ALL PATHS LEAD TO PRODUCT.

☐ 139 CHARITY

I don't know too many businesses that give out charity dollars for no reason. I've been on both sides of the coin and usually, businesses are looking for something. So even though it's marked up as charity, they want to get some sort of R.O.I. (return on investment) on it. It's usually some PR play, or there's an underlying reason.

As a matter of fact, if a business is doing something for no reason, you probably wouldn't hear about it. I've never worked for a company that writes checks and doesn't want anything from it. I have, however, worked with individuals that write checks and want nothing back.

Here's my encouragement: Spend some money. Save some money. Share some money.

☐ 140 MR. JONES

Have you heard of the singer Ben Folds? He wrote an amazing song called *Fred Jones Part 2*. It's about a job growing past a person and that person becoming obsolete. I see this it all the time in the work that I do—people failing to grow, failing to move forward, failing to innovate, not willing to change, and holding on to the past or what they're used to. I hope that I catch myself if I ever do this. If you ever see me do this, let me know because it so costly to business.

If you're turning your back on technology or disassociate yourself from the changing times of business, you're going to get left behind. We must innovate. We must remain raw at all times. Push yourselves. We are prime for this. We are being handed so many things. To those of you in your late 30s, 40s, 50s, 60s and up, don't disregard the growth of technology in your business.

Push yourself to use new tools in business because the second you start saying, "No, I'm not into that. Where are the typewriter stores? Where did all the typewriter stores go? Where do I get my typewriter fixed?" You're getting left behind.

☐ 141   GIVE

Do you believe in the bible? Do you believe in Buddha? Do you believe in Aristotle? Do you believe in Tom Cruise? All of those sources state that you have to give to receive. As a matter of fact, that is a very common theme in most religions.

Some people are adamant about keeping business secrets. They say, "That's what I do to make money. I can't tell others about my process, where to find business, or how to do this and that because that's what I do. They might steal my idea. They might use that concept instead of paying me to do it." Newsflash: Nobody's going to do that. In fact, by giving information away, you simply place yourself at the very top of your industry as an influencer. A leader. I know it seems counter-intuitive, but you must give to receive. You've got to give before you can ask to receive anything.

Give. People would rather pay you to do what you do, than to try and do it themselves. (That's why there is a landscaping industry. Nobody wants to mow their own lawn. Can I do it? Yeah, of course. But do I want to? No. Never. I never want to touch another lawnmower in my life.)

Take the next opportunity to freely share something you usually wouldn't because you think its proprietary to you or a trade secret. See what happens when you give.

☐ 142 BIRTHDAY

One day, back in my comedy club days, we decided to throw our own birthday party so everybody could come to thank us for being around for three years and providing great comedy to our community. So we did. We set up the event. We invited everybody we knew. Nobody showed up. You know why? Because our business is not for us.

Your business is not for you. It's for the people. They don't care if it's your birthday. They want comedy and beer. They want the product/service that you provide and they want it how they want it. I like seeing companies throw their own birthday parties, but the smart ones offer something to their customers to celebrate with them. They say, "It's our birthday and we got you a gift," or "Free night on us." I stood in line for half an hour once to get a Jimmy John's sub for a dollar. You know why it was one dollar? Because they were celebrating their birthday and me.

If you own your own company, realize that it is not for you—it is for the people. You might enjoy doing business and the money that comes in is yours, but your product or service, that's your customers'. Your business exists to give them that product or service.

If you're going to throw your own birthday party, maybe give everybody a gift. Say, "Hey, it's our birthday. Here, you can have something." Otherwise, people don't care that it's your birthday.

CEREAL

☐ 143   CHEVETTE

When I was about 14 or 15, my dad owned a cell phone shop. This is back when you had to install cell phones into your cars (I know, right? I just blew some of your minds!). They also installed radios and other electronics. Eventually, I became one of their installers. At the time, I had a 1983 Chevette. This car was old and beat. The radio in my car was probably worth about $25, and I traded the speakers for a skateboard.

I installed $1,000 radio systems into perfect, beautiful, $80,000 cars. My car? It had a $25 system. I say that to tell you this: A mechanic's car is always broken, and a maid's house is always dirty.

What service do you provide, and is it a service you should be providing to yourself? Let's all buckle down and make sure that, if we're mechanics, our cars aren't broken. If we're maids, our houses aren't dirty. If we build websites, make sure our own website looks good.

☐ 145   SHARE

I love social media marketing. The way we advertise on social media keeps changing—banners don't work, pop-ups don't work, Facebook sidebars don't work.

People ask me all the time what they should share. Everything. Share everything. Do you have a business? Did you get new pencils in the office? Share it. Share, share, share, share, content, content, content, content, content trumps quality.

If you have a business and you want to promote it, start sharing content. I don't care what it is, just share it. If you want to make that content even better, make it super transparent. Use it to tell your story

☐ 144   HAPPY

My first company toured the US and Europe in trains, planes, and automobiles, and performed comedy for churches, clubs, schools, camps. I, for some reason, had the wherewithal to make sure that I took the time to be present and happy with wherever I was. I can remember very distinctly, multiple times, saying "Let's just breathe this in. This is a really great time in life. This is amazing. I am happy now. I have goals, dreams, and ambitions that I want to achieve, but I am happy right now."

We can be so goal-oriented, so goal-driven, looking so far ahead, leaning so forward that we forget to be happy right now. Our goals could be financial stability, to go on a vacation, get married, or have kids. We're sometimes so focused on them and think that, when we get there, that's when we'll be happy. The truth is, when we get there, we'll realize that reward was in the journey.

I want to encourage you to be happy right now, in this moment. Be happy right where you are. This is a great time of life for you. You're going to look back and say, "That was a great time in life." You're going to want to look back and say, "Wow, I sure am glad that I stopped to smell the roses, take in the happiness, and be proud of myself for what I did."

☐ 146   CURRICULUM

To get a diploma, you have to graduate high school. To graduate high school, you have to pass a certain amount of classes with a certain grade. To reach that grade, you have to pass tests. Then to get through those tests, you have to work through a certain number of pages in textbooks. (I didn't really pay attention in high school. I think that's how it goes.) In school, to get to your final goal, which is your diploma, there is a set, standard path for you to take. Then, when you get out of school and if you want to start your own business, the path vanishes. There is no path. Every path is different. You're making it up yourself, and often times, people who are bad at starting businesses are bad at setting a path.

I've talked about business plans in other lessons in this book. We all know those are great, but they're living, breathing documents that ebb and flow. They often fail. Here's how to build your own curriculum that will get you to a diploma of running your first business:

1. Set a goal

For example: I want to sell a hundred widgets in my first year

2. Break it down

How many widgets is that a day? How many widgets do I have to sell in a day to get to 100? How many phone calls does it take for me to talk to business owners to sell a widget? You can break them all the way down to what you have to do in a single day. If you add those tasks up, they end up at your final goal.

Break down your goals right up to what you have to do within the hour. Let those hours be the pages you had to read in high school, or the exam you had to study for. Those days will start to add up, and lead to your secondary or tertiary goals, that finally end up reaching your primary goal.

Build your own curriculum that eventually graduates you to a successful company.

☐ 147 UNINSULT

We've all had this happen to us: You wake up one morning and you say, "I want this thing. I think this store sells this thing." You drive to the store and walk in, "I came here to get this thing," and the person at the store says, "Oh we don't have that in, but we can order it for you."

Here's my problem with "We can order it for you": It's insulting to a customer if you're going to tell them that your company can order what they want online—we know! In this day and age of online sales, the fact that we're walking into your store tells you that we want it right now.

Pay attention to your customer in such a way that you are not insulting them. Nobody in the history of business ever said, "Oh yeah, perfect, can you go order that for me. Then I'll just drive across town to come back here again. Why would I want it delivered to my house for a cheaper price? Yeah, sure, order that for me, I'll wait…"

Let's pay attention, so that we are not insulting our customers.

☐ 148 HUSTLEST

Some of the most successful people I've been around have this outrageous will to win. They have mastered the art of how to hustle. They're not the smartest, best looking, or the richest, but they hustle, hustle, hustle.

Check to see on a scale of 1 to 10, how much are you hustling? Are you hustling? Do you want it, and how much do you want it?

☐ 149   STATUS

One of the first things we teach in improv is that your status is above the crowd. If you watch any good comedian, they set that standard at the very beginning of the show. I'm going to give you what you asked for, what you paid for, but *I'm* running the show.

When you set up a relationship with a customer, you're setting up a status. You're declaring how the relationship will function. The best companies set the status up as, "I'm going to be the cool person in this relationship." When you go into an Apple store, do you feel like you're the coolest person in the store? No. That's because the status is set up right from the beginning that I (Apple), am going to be the cool person; I'm the one in control of this.

Yes, you are there to serve your customers and that's definite. But they're not going to be the cool person in the relationship; they're not going to be the ones calling the shots. You're calling the shots.

Set that status up in such a way that you are controlling the relationship with your customers.

☐ 150   ERROR

Why are we so afraid to fail? Why is it that the first thing we learn in school is that failing is bad? You get big F on your paper. You made an error. There are too many errors on your paper, your report has failed.

Most of us learn from trial and error. Very few of us learn from reading books. You can look at a map of how to get to Florida, but until you drive to Florida, you don't know what the journey will be like.

Next time you get a chance to bite off more than you can chew, do it. Do it because you're going to have errors, and you're going to learn, and you're going to try again, and you're going to win. Or maybe you'll make another error, but eventually, you will win. Trial and error. Error a lot.

☐ 151   UNLEARN

I've met many people who wrestle with notions that they've picked up along the way in life; ideas that are forced upon us by society and how we're raised—let's call them rules. For example, 40 hours a week is a work week; you don't have enough money to grow; or that you can't achieve something unless you have experience.

If there's one thing I know about business, especially people who have been successful, they forget the rules. They unlearn the rules they have been conditioned with. They're really good at it, too. It's like President John F. Kennedy saying that they're going to put a man on the moon. Do you know how ridiculous that was in the '60's? Ridiculous. That would be like saying today, "In the next 10 years, we're going to teleport." That is how ridiculous that was. But they achieved it—they put a man on the moon.

Are there any rules you're living by that you shouldn't be? What are you telling yourself that is complete bull? Examine some of the rules you're following but don't need to follow.

☐ 152   MILLENIALS

People often ask me about how to deal with millennials. I don't see any difference between millennials and any other generation (except for the Boomers, but nobody's like the Boomers). The advice I give to young people is not based on them being millennials, but on them being young people.

Most young people right now have the ability to make a lot of mistakes and learn quick. They don't have kids, they're not married, the economy is good (as it stands in late 2016). My advice is go out and make mistakes now while you can live in your parents' basement. You don't know what an advantage that is with the amount of time that you have. Don't follow the rule of "Focus."

I'm encouraging you, don't focus. Try everything. The one thing that lights you up, you won't have to worry about trying to focus on—it'll be all you'll ever think about.

☐ 153   NATIVE

I've written in other lessons in this book about millennials and how there is no difference from that generation to the next when it comes to marketing to them. In this lesson, I'm telling you that you should have a millennial on your marketing team. They're what we call "digital natives".

Anybody 18 and under doesn't know life without the internet. It's a digital world we're living in as entrepreneurs. Some of us are resistant to give in to the efficiencies that technology can provide because we're not comfortable.

Now I'm going to make you even more uncomfortable: Have a millennial on your team; at the very least, have a digital native. Talk to your daughter tonight. Ask her how she's using the internet, be it on her mobile device or at school. That's going to help you market because times, they are a-changing. If we're not ready, we're just going to get passed up.

☐ 154   NOW

I decided to be a triathlete later in my life. It seems like that's what a lot of people do. By no means am I the youngest person at these events, but I am on the younger side. As a matter of fact, the most competitive age category is the 40-year-old category. In my last race, there were six people who ran between the ages of 40 to 45, and five of them were in the top 20 (guess who one wasn't). HA!

What are you waiting for?

Remember, before you got married, you were like, "I just need the timing to be right to get married." It never really came around, but you got married? Remember when you started thinking about kids, "I've got to wait for the timing to be right." The timing never really came around, but you did it anyway. Why don't you start your own company? The timing is never going to be right. Just do it. Start it today. I hear a lot of people say they wish they could, but the only ones stopping them from doing it are themselves.

☐ 155   AMISH

There's a great part of Ohio, up in the northeast, known as Amish country. The Amish are great. They said goodbye to VCRs, microwaves, toaster ovens, and cars. They drive these little buggies around with a horse in front of it.

Now the Amish, figuratively and literally, put the horse before the cart. Ingrained into our heads, too, is this notion that we cannot put the cart before the horse. That saying doesn't really work anymore. Because we have technology, now more than ever is the perfect time to put the cart before the horse, in terms of starting your own business.

To test your concept, go out and see if it works. Use technology to do that because you're going to save a lot of money. Point, shoot, aim. Next time you get the opportunity, put the cart before the horse and see if it doesn't save you time and money.

☐ 156 LINES

If you're going to start a business, try and make it a business where you're making money while you sleep. (No, not from doing sleep tests. No, not from selling your morning breath.) Start a company where you're making money when you don't have to work. If you are a consultant and all you do is consult, then you're only making money when you consult.

Try adding a line of revenue that comes in while you're sleeping—memberships, subscriptions, merchandise, or videos—some way, some thing, some avenue, some arm that you could possibly be making sales while you're sleeping.

That's one of the biggest reasons to become an entrepreneur. So you can make money while you're not working.

☐ 157 RESPECT

Have you ever been asked to come to a meeting and, 15 minutes into the meeting, you realize why this meeting shouldn't have ever been called?

If you are calling a meeting with people, make sure that you have a plan. Make sure you have a roadmap for that meeting. Make sure that you appreciate the time of the people in that meeting. It makes them feel a lot better about dedicating their time to you.

☐ 158   SATURN

I was working with a client recently, and we've been harping on something called the Fun Zone. The Fun Zone is the place in which you are inside your core competencies and is life-giving to you. It's something you could do all the time, 24/7, and it would not get old. Usually with entrepreneurs, we do three things really well and then everybody else does the rest. But we really love doing those three things. (I discuss more about enjoying your Fun Zone in Lesson 77 "MEANDER".)

Here's how I picture it:

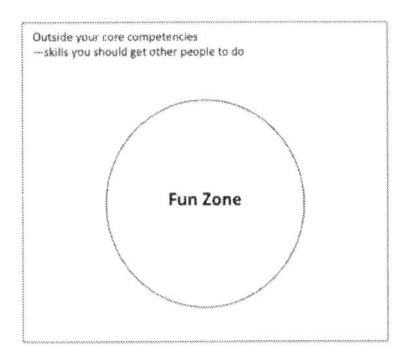

[Diagram: A square labeled "Outside your core competencies —skills you should get other people to do" containing a circle labeled "Fun Zone"]

But I have yet another theory:

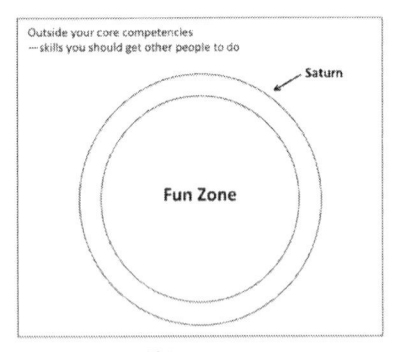

[Diagram: A square labeled "Outside your core competencies —skills you should get other people to do" containing two concentric circles. The inner circle is labeled "Fun Zone" and the ring between the circles is labeled "Saturn"]

I'm finding that there's this extra circle, like Saturn, that's outside your core competencies' Fun Zone, but inside the things you do well—**it's the things you do well but you don't like to do.** These things are just as important as the core competencies inside the Fun Zone.

Here's an example: I'm really great at basketball. I can do it. I can shoot. I can score. I can box out. I can run. I can jump. I can do all that, but I don't like to play basketball. I don't want to ever play basketball. It never seems appealing to me. In regards to business, one of those things for me is sales. I don't like to do sales. I don't think it's fun. However, I do it very well.

I want to encourage you to see what's just outside of your Fun Zone; the things you are good at doing but don't like to do. Challenge yourself to push through and do those things. We don't want to spend too much time doing them, but there are times when you're going to have to.

☐ 159   TWO

Because of my startup, I find myself asking for leads from people around me. "What kind of person are you looking for?" I say, "The breathing kind."

This is why: I know the demographic I'm looking for to sell my product. I know that any person is only two people away from the person I want to sell to. I can network myself to anyone I want, and so can you. You are two connections away from the person you want to talk to. All you need is two introductions.

So when somebody asks you, "Hey, I'd like to help your business out. Whom can I introduce you to?" Say, "Someone who's breathing," because that's two people away from whom you want to talk to.

☐ 160 INNOVATE

Do you remember that girl or guy in high school that you wanted? Oh my gosh, if you could just get your chance to be with that person, to call them girlfriend or boyfriend. You pay attention to see who she likes. She likes football players so you try out for the football team. Remember trying to be somebody you weren't so you could get the girl/boy?

Often times in business, I see clients doing the exact, same thing. Revenue or profit's down so they think they need to do something different so that they can make money. They start looking around to see what's working and they try to mimic that. Only to find out that it doesn't often work like that, as a matter of fact, I've never seen it work like that. What works is companies that constantly innovate, tear down their walls, and build them back up again when things stop working.

Ask yourself this question: Are you imitating to make money or are you innovating to be a leader in your industry? Innovation is all about breaking things. It's not just about building things up. It's about trying and failing. It's about failing and failing and failing until you get it right. The next time you feel like imitating so that you can raise revenue, tear down the walls instead. Tear them all down and build them back up again. Innovate, be a leader.

☐ 161 VERTS

Do all us entrepreneurs need to be extroverts? NO.

If you're telling your story, pitching your business, looking for investors, for people to join your team or buy your product—you pick your song, you sing it, you use your authentic voice and you sell it.

The only difference, in this case, between being an introvert or extrovert, is that at the end of the day, introverts will feel depleted and have a need to recharge. Extroverts will be thirsty for more.

☐ 162 MANUAL

I was once on a panel on what it's like to be a "boot-strapper". One thing it reminded me of was the necessity for proof of concept.

I was talking with a lady and she was telling me about a mobile application she wanted to build. It sounded really cool. She started talking about developers and everything that it would take to get things going. Then I said, "What if you built the whole thing but it doesn't work like you imagined, or there's no market for it?" I suggested that she run her app manually. That suggestion sounds highly inefficient, but for the first two customers that would be okay. I knew she'd get a chance to see if it could work or not.

Do you have a concept? Do you have a business idea? Before you spend money, try to prove that concept manually. Then once you have proof of concept it's easier to get money for that concept.

☐ 163 STAGES

How are you growing your influence? Where is your stage?

Where are you growing your influence? Are you building your stage and then performing from it? What are you doing on your stage? How are you promoting you? Why would you want to?

The best business card you could ever have is a client/customer/friend who already knows you and how good you are at what you do. This is why you want a stage. The audience is finding out how good you are at what you do.

When you work with one person, only that one person knows how good you are at what you do. If you do what you do in front of thousands of people, they all figure out how good you are at what you do. If you're good at what you do (and you should be, or you should move on), you need to be building stages in front of larger amounts of people and build that trust between you, your clients, potential clients, or customers. I can't tell you how many times people have come to me from watching my video blogs:

"Chip, I know you don't know me but I watch your vlogs. I need to hire you to do this thing."

My vlogs aren't my only stage, but they're probably my biggest stage. It's my main focus. I love doing it, it's fairly easy to do, and it helps me build trust and transparency with my clients.

☐ 164 SPEND?

How do you justify spending money in your company? How do you know when it's time to spend money?

I have two answers:

1. If you want to spend money, you're a lot like me. I love spending money and buying stuff, at the very highest rate too. I always pay top dollar for the thing I want because I want it now.

2. The real me, the one who makes smart decisions, spends money when it's absolutely necessary.

Which one are you? Do you have trouble holding back when it's time to hold back? I know I do. Here's a good test: Say you want something for your business. How quickly will that thing pay for itself? Does it have a chance to not pay for itself? If yes, then don't buy it.

If you want to buy something for your company, which you *think* you need, don't buy it. If you want to buy something for your company that you *know* you need, you have proof that it'll get used, and you have proof that it'll turn into money, then go buy it. Use it. Don't hesitate.

☐ 165   OLD

Did I do enough? Did I run outside and kiss the rain under electrical skies? Did I remember to say cheers? Did I at least try to kiss the prettiest girl at the right time? - Alkaline Trio

This morning on the way to drop my daughter Zoie off, we had an interesting conversation.

Zoie: You've been alive for 41 years.

Chip: I have been alive for 41 years. Is that a lot?

Zoie: Yeah.

Chip: Yeah, you've only been alive for six years. Mom is 36.

Zoie: She will be 36?

Chip: She'll be 36 in ten days. Pretty cool, huh?

Zoie: Yeah.

When you're young, life doesn't seem that long. You just can't imagine life past 30 or 40. When I turned 40, I was slapped in the face with my mortality. Holy moly. I'm halfway done.

But this year, I turned 41. Something weird happens. Holy crap, that was 40 years? At the very least, Lord willing, I have 40 more of those? Holy moly. Life is long.

To everybody under 30, life is a lot longer than you think. You will have multiple careers. Stop thinking that you're only going to have one or two careers. You're going to have six or seven careers. Don't be afraid to shift. Don't be afraid to get outside of your comfort zone. Don't be afraid of what people are going to say to you if you decide to change your mind.

I get so mad when people get mad at people for changing their mind. "They can't settle on something." Good! You don't want to settle, you want to be revived, alive, enthralled. You want to stay up all night thinking about it. There are no rules. The business pioneers realized that really early on. There are no rules.

☐ 166   QUIT

A client asked me, "Here's my business idea, what do you think?" I told him what he wanted to hear, but then I told him what I wanted to say after that, "Ideas are a dime a dozen, it's how you execute."

I've said that before, but here's something I'm saying that's new: It's not only how you execute, it's also what you have in here (chest)! Is there any 'quit' in you at all? Open up. Look inside yourself and if you find a little bit of 'quit' in there, don't do it. But, if there's no 'quit' in any ounce of your body, do it. Go do it.

In entrepreneur circles, you see this graph often:

Your Plan

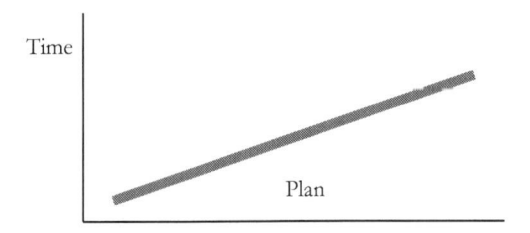

Your Realistic Plan (see curved line)

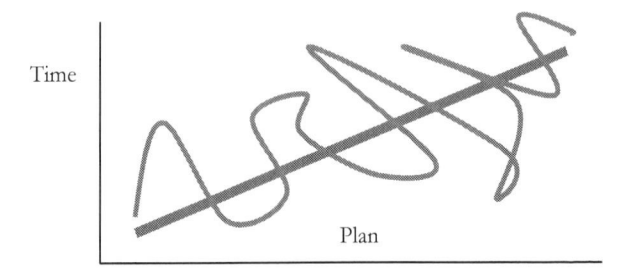

Don't start a business unless you're willing to walk through the curved, topsy-turvy line. Are you ready for your life to be super tough until the very last minute when you win? That could happen if you choose the entrepreneur life.

☐ 167 OWNER

The day and age of being an owner of a small company—i.e. under $5 million in revenue, under 50 employees, owner of that company not being a public figure—are over. If you're running your company and are having trouble being the center of attention with the content that you're putting out, you're going to be at a major disadvantage.

Content is king and to create that content, you need to be part of it. People want to know the story of the company, and you're in it, owner. If you have a company and you're having trouble producing content that you're involved in, it's time to get over it. People want to know who you are. People want to know where the company started, how it started. Who are you? Who are they giving their money to?

If you're having trouble creating the content, get somebody to hang around you and create the content for you. Content is king.

☐ 168   80-20

Today's magic word is "numbers". Yay!

As an entrepreneur you're going to be familiar with a lot of numbers. 1099, W-9, area codes, zipcodes, etc. But there are two numbers you're going to find popping up everywhere and that is 80 and 20. Or 20 and 80.

These are percentages. It is how things work. 20 percent of what you do is going to account for 80 percent of the outcome. 20 percent of the people you hire will do 80 percent of the work. Be aware of that going into business. There's no way to get around it. 20-80. You're going to do 100 percent of the work but 20 percent of that work is going to account for 80 percent of the outcome.

As you go into projects, keep in mind only 20 percent of this work is going to be worth it. But the other 80 is how you get to that 20. Don't give up. Don't be surprised by the outcomes.

☐ 169 YOUT'

There are a lot of benefits to teaching a youth about entrepreneurship. One is that when you give youth the chance to run a business, you get to see a different side of them, a side they might not get to use if they didn't have the opportunity to run something. Not everybody is built to work under somebody. Some of us are built to be at the top, to be the decision maker, to be the creator, to be the guide.

When you give a kid a chance to run a company, you give them a chance to see if their skillset falls in line. With that comes better self-esteem, a sense of accomplishment, and responsibility. Now, one out of 10, or maybe even one out of a 100, will end up actually running their own company, but they at least deserve a chance.

Something we throw around a lot in my entrepreneurial circle is that an entrepreneur without guidance is just a criminal. If we can get these kids to have some entrepreneurial guidance early on, we'll give them the chance to do well and feel accomplished.

Are you around youth that would benefit by learning how to run their own company? You might be saving them a lot of heartache and confusion if you just gave them the chance to see what it feels like to call the shots.

☐ 170 PLAN C

In the '60's, they wanted to put a man on the moon. They did everything they could, all the analysis, the data collection, they built cool rockets, calculated the science—estimations, projections, equations. Even after all that, they still didn't know exactly what was going to happen once the lunar module landed. As a matter of fact, if their calculations were right, there should have been so much dust on the moon that they wouldn't have been able to land. There would have been hundreds and hundreds of feet of dust. As we know, in hindsight, there were only four to five inches.

With my start up, Perkbird, we did all the calculations and analyses on how the launch would go but we still couldn't exactly tell what was going to happen. Plan A didn't work, Plan B is not working, but Plan C worked terrifically.

You can have all your plans, all the data, all the analyses, and it could all still be wrong. So keep pushing on, keep trying, keep coming up with plans, and just like they landed a man on the moon, your business will succeed, eventually.

☐ 171 SYNONYMOUS

If you want new customers, you have to market, and if you're going to market, you have to advertise. There are a lot of ways to advertise—events, print, radio, me, social media, email campaigns—but whatever you do, you have to throw something out there. Most of the time, you're advertising some sort of a deal. Now, here's the catch. When you say you're having a sale or that you're discounting something, customers might get the wrong impression.

For instance, one day I had the bright idea of hiring a sign spinner at the comedy club. The spinner was out there flipping the sign around. (It was awesome! And so cool!) But then I started getting questions like, "Are you going out of business?" Sometimes people think that a sale is synonymous with there being something wrong in our business. To fix that problem, you need to find some way to get your name out there, and not lead with the "discount".

What is it saying when you are putting on a sale? Sometimes it is saying that you're just putting on a sale because you want to, sometimes it's saying desperation. There's a very thin line to walk there.

☐ 172   S&P

If you're interested in scaling your business which is highly, highly connected to you and your abilities, you better start thinking about how are you going to recreate yourself.

Have you ever watched "The Terminator"? When The Terminator came out, the movie's whole concept was unimaginable. Crazy. We would never have robots that would take over the world. In this day and age, that's not such a crazy concept. I mean we're not at that stage and I don't fear robots, but we're getting close to duplicating ourselves.

Say you have a business, and it starts doing well. That's because you're good at what you do. Challenge over, right? No, because your business starts growing, and you can't do everything, but the influx of customers is still coming.

Here's where the new challenge is: How do you duplicate yourself so that you can scale your company? You can't make more money unless you can accept more business. You can't accept more business unless there is more of you. You need to be able to duplicate yourself. It's a talent that all truly great leaders have.

I call it "monkeyfying" your company. What does that mean? People aren't monkeys, but if you can make your company simple enough to run that a monkey can do it, then you win. You do that through Systems and Processes. S and Ps. Monkeyfy your business with S and Ps. How do you answer the phone? I hit this, say this, they usually say that, and then I respond with this—that is a system. You do it every time. Show that path to somebody. Monkeyfy your company.

If you do scale, *you* handle premium customers. For the rest of the customers, they can come in to the staff that you hired and trained through systems and processes. Will they make more mistakes than you? Yes. Will they attract less business than you? Yes. Will you get more business in the long run? Absolutely. So if you want to scale your business, monkeyfy it with systems and processes.

☐ 173   YES'

Today, I walked into an insurance agent's office. There were two agents in there. I told them that I wanted to tell them about my startup company and that it was built to help them. As the first guy moved around me to start to walk out, he stopped to listen to my pitch, standing in the doorway. Then he said, "I'm not interested." The other agent took the cue from that and said, "I'm not interested, either." I said, "Well, then you have to let me out that door," as the one agent was standing directly in the doorway.

Both of them didn't know what to say. I think they were taken aback by how quickly I was onto the next stop.

If you're selling something and someone says, "No," move on. Of course, for every one out of every 50 no's you're going to get a yes, but think about how much time you save by moving on to the next person to get to the "yes"?

Get to the "yes"! Everything else in between is just slowing you down.

☐ 174   10

Today I knocked on a door, walked in, but there wasn't anybody at the front desk. A lady poked her head out.

"Can I help you?"

"Yes, my name is Chip, I'm here from Portland to talk to insurance agents about my startup company, Perkbird. Could I have five minutes?"

"No, but you can have 10 seconds."

I was able to explain to her in 10 seconds what it is that Perkbird does in such a way that she sat there and talked to me for about half an hour. Had I not been able to explain Perkbird in 10 seconds, I would have lost her.

When you are trying to bring a business in, you need to be able to explain that company really quickly. I don't care how convoluted your process is, how neat your company is, or how dynamic it is. You have to say what is does very quickly.

Take time in the next couple of days to say what it is that your company does in 10 seconds. See if you can cover the whole thing in 10 seconds. You're going to need that, maybe not everyday, but one day you're going to get a "You have 10 seconds, go!," and you'll have something ready that works.

☐ 175 NO-ING

There's a stigma: "I can't go into sales because what if people say "No?""

There's this weird concept out there where many believe that sales is selling things. Sales is mostly not selling anything. 95 percent of the time, you don't sell anything. It's like fishing—most of the time you don't catch anything, but they don't call it catching, they call it fishing.

Sales shouldn't be called sales; it should be called "Having people say "No" to you," because you're not selling. Mostly, people are saying no to you.

Sales is mostly you walking around, talking to people, dealing with people that aren't into what you're selling. I mean, how could you expect everybody to buy what you're selling? You would be Facebook at that point. But even Facebook, I'm sure, early on, had people say, "No. Not into it. Not going to work. Not going to do it. Leave me with Myspace."

If you're in sales, change it to "Getting told No." Eventually you're going to get those "Yes"'. And those are the people that you raise up, foster, harbor, grow, love. But those are few and far between.

☐ 176   BOOST

My mom taught me how to drive. She gave me lots of great advice, some of which I still use to this day. One of the lessons I remember most is, "If you're sitting in a turn lane, waiting to turn left crossing traffic, don't turn your steering wheel before you take off because if somebody rear ends you while your waiting, and your wheel is already turned, you will shoot into the oncoming traffic and get into an accident.

If, all of the sudden, you were to get a boost in the direction of your steering wheel, would it be in a direction that you would like to go? If you would, then perfect. If you wouldn't, let's change the direction of our steering wheel, so that when that boost does hit us, we'll end up going where we want to go.

☐ 177   PRODUCT

Somebody came to me with a product they wanted to develop. They showed me how it worked, told me the name of it, their plans for marketing it, and then they asked what everybody does at the end.

"What do you think?"

I did what I always do, I told them what they want to hear, "I think it's a great idea." Then I told them what I wanted to say:

It is not the value of a product or service but the amount of work you're willing to put into it. What's behind your idea? What's your story?

It's not the product that people are buying, it's the story. It's what they're belonging to when they trade currency for your product or service.

Concepts are awesome, ideas are really cool. Do research, find out if there's something like it out there. There might be, there might not be. But in the long run, it's you and the amount of work you're willing to put behind it that matters.

It's not how smart you are (although that helps). It's not how much money you have (although that helps). It's not how cool the product or service is (although that helps). It's you and how much work you're willing to put in. How many days are you willing to get up in the morning and work really hard for what you want?

☐ 178   MIDDLE

I'm afraid there is going to be a major change in a very common phrase that a lot of people believe in. I know this because sometimes I can tell the future. "Work smarter, not harder" is not true.

I hate to break it to you. It's bad news for some of you. It's bad news for some of you with low energy levels. It's bad news for some of you who are not ADHD. It's bad news for some of you who prefer to get things easier.

You have to work smarter AND harder.

One of my favorite marketers, Gary Vaynerchuk, has this saying that he refers to a lot, "Everything is clouds and ground". He works in the clouds or on the ground. That's right. You have to work smarter at the top, and then harder at the bottom.

With my startup, Perkbird, we had all these plans, but only two of them were working. Guess which ones those were? The clouds and the ground.

The clouds: Meeting with a lot of influential people in our regions.

The ground: Door to door sales.

You know which plan didn't work? The middle, i.e. networking meetings, etc.

If you're leading a project, the best place for you to be is in the clouds and on the ground.

☐ 179   #1

I went to the San Diego Startup Week and attended a talk called Stuff Founders Don't Want To Talk About.

The panelists were asked, "What was one big mistake that you made, or what is the biggest thing you would tell a founder?" An answer that struck me, from one of the panelists, was that companies exist for the family, not vice versa. He said it very simply and I loved it.

We've been conditioned to think, from a young age, that you have to go to work so that you can support your family, then a weird thing can happen where all of a sudden your passion takes over and you can forget that you're doing this for your family.

What you're doing is for your family. Your family is #1. If what you're doing is taking you away from your family, maybe it's time to readjust.

☐ 180   OUT

If you're trying to develop your business, most of the game is really just being out there. Just get out. Move, shake. The best way to do that is to serve people. Get them a gift. Buy them lunch. Buy them coffee. Show up with a coffee. You don't know if they drink coffee or not, but show up with it. What's the worst that could happen? My $2 coffee gets thrown away. Big whoop.

Ask people. Ask for leads, connections. Ask them how you can help them and then tell them how they can help you. You can't do that from behind a phone or a desk.

☐ 181   COMFORT

While I was in San Diego on a Perkbird scouting trip, I wore the same shirt almost everyday because I was having so much luck with it. I'm not superstitious, but I do know when I feel comfortable. If I feel comfortable with me, then I think everybody else does, and that's important.

Do you feel comfortable? Obviously, we need to have some sort of a dress code. We can't be rude to people, can't show up in their office with shorts on.

What are we doing besides dress that makes us feel comfortable?

There are a lot of ways to get comfortable: Lucky shirt, studying up on your clients, or showing up super early for a meeting.

How do you get comfortable for your meetings? If you get comfortable, they're going to be comfortable.

☐ 182   VALUE

As service providers, we can be tempted to discount our service so that we can get business. Here are two things you can do with your price when you're wanting to win more business:

1. You can lower your price
2. You can raise your price

Next time you feel tempted to lower your price, go to the person who wants you to lower it and show them what you'd have to take away from your offer to meet the price they are looking for.

What you're providing has more value than you think.

☐ 183   UN-ENFUEGO

When we're out there doing our thing as entrepreneurs, trying to do our best, sometimes we get stuck. Sometimes we might lose our edge for a really long time. We lose that fire. We become un-enfuego. I'm here to show you a source of inspiration that you might not have used yet.

In the summer of 2016, I started running triathlons. When you enter a triathlon, they write your number on one calf and your age on the other. Need inspiration? Start looking at the age of the people running past you. Most people were older than me. Yikes!

If you need inspiration with your entrepreneurial effort, look around you. You'll see people who are where you want to be. The only way they got there was by really hard work and a little bit of luck. Mostly really hard work and some natural ability. But mostly really hard work.

Open your eyes. Inspiration is all around you. You can be inspired to do better by the things that are right within your grasp.

☐ 184   MICRO

I love the show Dirty Jobs. Do you know that show? The host's name is Mike Rowe. I'm a big fan of his, but recently there's a video circulating around of him talking about why you should not follow your dreams and how you should find a passion within the job that you have. Sorry Mike Rowe, I just couldn't disagree more.

If that were the case, the USA would never be the USA that it is today. If our forefathers would have said, "Let's just stick around here and deal with all the crap that people are giving us because we don't want to chase our dreams of freedom," we would never be this country today.

I want to encourage you to follow your dreams and your passions, not because that's the cool thing to say. It's the one thing that I look for in somebody whom I want to work with. It's the one thing that people who are good at hiring look for. Is there a passion? Are you doing what you love? Otherwise, you're going to give a half-assed effort.

I had lunch with my buddy who works at LinkedIn. LinkedIn just allowed their employees take as many vacation days as they like. That works for them because the people that they hire have a passion for LinkedIn's mission, which is to connect people to good jobs. When you have a passion for your job, you might take a week or two off but you're not going to go take six months off. You would be too worried about the projects that you were on.

Follow your passions and your dreams or else people are going to see through you.

☐ 185　　DOOR

Going door to door, getting shut down, being stood up. That's all right. It all leads up to a victory. The win. We will always win as long as we don't quit.

Here's a perfect example: I had just shot the first bit of a vlog about "not quitting". It had been a long day of going door to door in San Francisco pitching Perkbird and a long day of "NO's". I shut off my phone. Got out of the car. Walked into my next stop. This was not a warm lead. They didn't even know I was coming. After a quick pitch, they were in. They loved it. They talked to me for about a half an hour. I walked them through the product demo, and had them look at the product. They loved it, and kept me in there for an hour. They gave me some water. They sent me connections, and got me going. They walked me out. Shook my hand. Said they're excited to use it. That's a win.

You win if you just keep going. You will win.

☐ 186　　VACATION

To those of you wanting to be entrepreneurs or starting to be entrepreneurs, especially serial entrepreneurs, the journey is going to be up and down and will, by far, be the hardest thing you'll ever do (besides raising kids). This is not just a message of warning, but of positivity.

When you're in your passion zone, your Fun Zone, your body will take over. Rely on that. Take care of it while you're going through it. Your body will give you the energy you're looking for. If you're not in your Fun Zone, I would recommend not getting yourself in a position where you're pressing yourself to the limits.

187 COMMUNITY

I got an email explaining why a business was not going to use Perkbird. They went on and on about how it was just easier to give their customers cash as a token of appreciation.

The person in this email went on to say that Perkbird should work with larger chain stores. Well, national chains are usually right next door or close to a single-owner local business in your community. Buying from them means that the money you spend goes back into your community.

Are you taking a holistic look at your business and the community that your business functions in? A flock of geese fly better together. The point of Perkbird is not to help companies reward their client, or to help companies get new business (although it does this very efficiently); the point of my company is to help a community of business owners work together better and grow faster because they're growing together. Is your business doing that? Do you have an eye for community or are you focused elsewhere?

☐ 188 SCALE

Have you reached that point in your business where you can't decide where the extra money should go—does it go to you or to your company? It's hard to know what to do with that extra money. Here are some pointers, in Do and Don't form:

DO: Scale

Hire another person and make sure they're better than you. When that works out, you'll start gaining money again. Hire another person and then another person and then another person. Hire people that are better than you. They're out there, they're amazing.

DON'T: Not scale, for fear of losing control of your company

Fear of losing control of your company is a bad thing. Guess what? It's not going to happen if you hire people that are better than you.

☐ 189   PASSION

My wife and I were talking about the assortment of opportunities that were placed in front of me when we relocated from San Diego, California to Salem, Oregon in 2009. We also talked about how glad we were that I didn't pick something I didn't have a passion for when I was starting a new chapter—we decided together that I would remain a serial entrepreneur.

When you're in the thick of making choices like these, it may seem like your spouse is upset or uncomfortable with such decisions because you're choosing to be bit more risky inside your passion area. It might seem a little rough at times, but you might be surprised by how supportive your spouse can be with this type of path.

If you get the a chance to do something in your career that might change the family dynamic, err towards the side of your passion, because in the long run everybody is going to be happier.

☐ 190   1 YEAR

Why did I commit to making daily vlogs? Here are my Top 5, but there are a lot more reasons.

1. It puts me out there. I preach it, so I have be it. Everyday that you go to work, minus my vacation, I am vlogging. Put yourself out there.

2. I am a very social person and people aren't always around me. It's nice that I get to talk to people through the camera.

3. It's a discipline. I have to do it. It feels good to complete something that you say you're going to.

4. I like the art of it. I like editing. It's an artistic outlet.

5. I get to meet and talk to a lot of people. I like helping people. I take great pleasure in helping people. You deserve it! I like doing it.

☐ 191   RE-UP

Remember the last day of school? One of the weird traditions on the last day of school was to walk out throwing papers everywhere (you can tell I'm from Florida because of our weird traditions). It was a big celebration. It was the end of the school year, and you were free for the summer to go out and have fun.

After finishing my first year of vlogging, I remember it feeling like the last day of school. In my own little way, I went out and threw papers in the air, but I also checked in with the goals I had made earlier, set some new ones, and got going. I re-up'd, if you will.

Take some time today to go back and take a look at the goals you've set. Where are you? Did you achieve them already? Should you re-up? Are you nowhere close? Should you double down? Re-up or double down? (That is the name of my next rap song, Re-Up Or Double Down?)

☐ 192 LONELY

If you don't like to be around people, then entrepreneurship is probably for you because you spend a lot of time, a long time, alone. As I sit here, thinking about how lonely entrepreneurship is, I don't mean to romanticize entrepreneurship. To those who are not entrepreneurs and have not started their own company, they might say that they know exactly what I do. They see all the fun parts of it, but what they don't see are the times of solitude. Patching dry wall, taking out the trash, building tables, desks, chairs, stages, bars, answering emails, writing proposals, driving, etc.

I think if you asked any entrepreneur if they could do anything other than what they currently do, they would pick something with more people around them because the things we do are so by ourselves. I think this is why people who consider themselves jack of all trades make good entrepreneurs. We have to do it all. There's no one else to do it. "How'd he learn how to do that?" I didn't have an option. I like having my vlog because with it I do have somebody here with me that has watched my entrepreneurship and seen how it's a lonely endeavor.

Entrepreneurship is lonely, but it doesn't have to be. There are ways around it. Entrepreneurship is like what I imagine mountain climbing to be. You're so excited to be a mountain climber, then you get on the mountain and you start climbing and everything's fine and dandy. Then you start to realize you're all alone and maybe you're not as brave as you thought you were and you get scared, but in the end, you make it to the top. Entrepreneurship has many hurdles, and loneliness is one of the biggest.

☐ 193   NOT SO LONELY

In 2015, I started a co-working space by the name of Co.W. It has been an amazing run. I've met so many people and gotten to work with so many cool companies. When we opened, I made sure we had really fast internet, cool desks, we were in a cool area of town, we had cool events, and we were known for a lot of really cool things. We also have a pet giraffe. (OK, we don't.) One of the cool things we have done is our Morning Meetup every Monday at 9:12 a.m.. Every member of Co.W who wants to, shows up at the conference room. Together, we go around the table and work on problems we're dealing with professionally.

This, by far, has been the most incredible piece of Co.W, because now I am not alone. Entrepreneurship is very lonely, but it doesn't have to be. Now, I have a group of friends with whom I go to work with almost every day and are interested in what I'm going through.

If you're an entrepreneur or thinking about being one—set up a group of people that you trust, feel comfortable with, and are interested in you, not just themselves, to come together. Having a group like this will help you surround yourself with people who are positive and encourage you. More importantly, this will also be an intentional group of people that you come to at a specific time every week and work on the issues you're all going through.

I challenge you to do this. Watch what happens almost immediately. It's incredible how quickly you will experience positive changes within your profession.

☐ 194   F STAGE

Think of your spouse or your significant other, the one that you've been with for a long time. Remember when you first started dating and things were going well, you were about a month or two in, and then that moment comes when your eyes meet and the moment is just right…and it happens. You fluff for the first time in front of your significant other. Remember yourself asking, "Is this going to go well? I don't know. I mean, everybody fluffs," and then at that moment, the seal is broken. You're at the Fart Stage with your significant other.

Now, think about your clients. Here's a way to avoid the dreaded "bad client situation"—that client you just want to get rid of, should never have taken anyways, and don't want to be around. You are frustrated with them; they're hard to work with; you want to just fire them. Before you come together as client and company, make sure that you are to the Fart Stage together—that stage where things are close, where you can say or do things around each other, and it feels comfortable. This will save you so much time.

So many clients whom you end up not wanting to work with would have never made it to the Fart Stage. Warning: Make sure they stay at the Fart Stage. You don't want anything past that. You don't want to work for mom and dad! You don't want to work for your neighbor down the street who you played poker with and went jet skiing together.

Just at the Fart Stage, not super buddy-buddies, not these-are-strangers-I-don't-know-them-at-all, but right in the middle. Fart Stage.

☐ 195   DRIVE

I love cars. America loves cars. We all love our cars. They're fun. Americans like to drive.

What drives you? What is driving you right now?

Do you want to buy a boat, and so you go to work and you make money so you can put some of that away? Do you want a big house? Do you want things? Do you want stuff? Or is it the game that drives you? Is it the constant shucking and jiving and pitching and rolling and turning and dipping and ins and outs? Chess moves. Checkers moves. Connect 4 moves. Is it the plotting and strategizing? Is that what drives you?

Are you driven by your passion for things or are you driven by your passion to do good work? Or are you not driven at all?

☐ 196   LIES

Do you remember meeting somebody you liked in high school and really wanting date them? You walked up to them and said, "Hi. I heard your name was Susan. I'm Chip. Nice to meet you." And then you said weird things like, "I heard your dad killed a guy." WHY did you say that? But somewhere along the way, you get to the stage where you learned how to play it cool (I never got to this stage BTW). "Hey babe. What's up? How you doin'?" You gained confidence! You weren't arrogant, but you had confidence. And then maybe your crush started to like you but you played the game a little bit. You were cool, confident, you didn't play too many games but you rested on the fact that she/he liked you.

Sales is like that. You can tell when somebody likes what you're selling and at that point, you're not really selling it, you're just repeating things they're saying. Like, "I love this. This is a great idea." "Yes it is. I totally agree. This is totally a great idea." Or, "This is a great thing you've got here." "Yeah I know, it is. It is a great thing." When you find yourself repeating things like that, you know you have somebody on your team and you should stop selling it. Don't say dumb stuff! Get to where you need to be and then get out of there before you turn them off or give them a reason to doubt you.

Deliver. Be honest. Be yourself. Have fun with it. Enjoy the people you're talking to, but when the sale is done, get out of there. Bow, say thank you, and get off the stage. They'll like you and they'll keep liking you because you didn't have a chance to lie to them. Don't give yourself a chance to lie to them.

☐ 197   PLAY

The shower effect

When you have your head so far deep in so many projects that sometimes you can't see the forest for the trees, and you get in the shower to take your mind off something. Then answers to problems you were trying to solve magically pop up.

Importance of play

Play has creativity and competition. It has joy and happiness. These are all good things to help clear your mind and revitalize that really smart part of your brain that solves problems, has great ideas, executes, and keeps an even-keeled temper. It re-energizes the batteries that work that part of your brain.

Take some time not only to detach from your work but also Play. Join a softball league, play poker, find something fun. Go roller-skating. Take an improv class. Lick one of those poisonous frogs and see where that takes you. Go to a comedy show. Pick a fight with a biker. Write a song. Shave your beard. Sing Kumbaya in the mall at the top of your lungs wearing a Speedo. Take your pick. You'll thank yourself for it.

☐ 198   SURF

I learned how to surf as I was growing up in Florida. I loved surfing and still do. One of the things I like about it is that you're using nature to create movement. There are several types of surfers: Fast, aggressive, slow, melodic, and everyone in between. Some surfers behave like they're mad at the wave—they really go at it. Others just try to use the wave by creating momentum started with their hands and then they ride on that wave, using that momentum. Just cruising.

I've also observed these types in business. You're creating momentum with your hands, doing a lot of toiling and working and paddling. Some of the best entrepreneurs have the skill of staying out in front of that momentum, not relaxing so that it passes you by, but also not really leaning forward so that you burn out and run out in front of the wave. It's like riding that middle section. It's a fine art, just like surfing.

☐ 199   SURF II

How do you sustain that momentum? Here are three ways:

1. Stay focused

The bad thing about surfing is that you can't do it at night because you can't see the waves. Always be looking at the goal. The main thing needs to stay the main thing. Stay focused.

2. Stay organized

When you're surfing, you really need to have everything together. Your leash needs to be on right. The wax needs to be on right. The fins need to be on right. Things need to be organized.

3. Appreciation

You didn't get in front of that wave by yourself. Thank the people around you for the hard work that they put in for you.

☐ 200 BAD DAYS

I've been learning to be present in the moment. If I'm stuck in traffic, I'm in traffic. I can do very little about it. It's funny, but when we have big victories, we celebrate. We have fun. I'd even encourage that, for sure. At the same time, if things are going bad, give yourself permission to feel bad and upset. If you're like me, there's no hiding your feelings. I wear them on my sleeve. Even when I try to hide them, people say to me, "Hey, you're having a bad day, aren't you?" Yes. I'm just no good at hiding them.

By owning your bad day, full-on admitting, owning it, and being in a bad mood, it allows you to go through the process quicker. Yeah, I'm in a bad mood. Let's get out of it. Stop by a client's office, see if they can cheer you up. Go on a drive. Go on a ride. Go for a swim. Go exercise. Go snipe hunting. Do something. Get it to run its course faster. It happens when you celebrate, right? "Yay, we did good! Alright, back to work."

Own your bad days. Get through them. Speed up the process.

☐ 201 CONSISTENT

Is there something that you are committed to doing daily? It's funny how easy yet difficult consistency can be. I watched a documentary on a guy who decided to take a picture of himself every hour for a year. It's funny how that mundane task is so easy but so hard.

Consistently be good with your customer service. Consistently show up early to meetings. Deliver a consistent product. Be consistent in your dress. Be consistent in your vocabulary. Add value to the projects you're working on by being consistent. It's so easy and so hard all at the same time, but it adds so much value to the thing that you are being consistent about.

Even when you don't want to, be consistent. Even when it takes all of your energy, and all of your might, be consistent.

☐ 202   FRIENDS

Remember that time in high school—why do all my stories start this way? I think my next book is going to be titled I Learned All I Need to Learn About Business in High School.

Remember when you started talking to this girl or guy, it was going well but it was weird how well you were hitting it off, only to find out that this person was using you to get to your best friend? How did that make you feel? Probably like a piece of poo-poo.

As you grow your business and things are going well, you may want to appoint brand ambassadors—people who really like your product or service. Yes, they are essential to you growing, but you want to be sure not to just use them like they're a piece of meat. This goes back to why I think it's so important that you only work with people you would hang out with. When somebody you wouldn't hang out with becomes your brand ambassador, you will have to hang out with somebody you don't want to. You'd be stuck.

If you choose to have a brand ambassador, choose somebody you want to hang out with. All you have to do is be friends with them. You definitely have to keep it professional, but at the same time if you're treating them as a friend, then you'll be thinking about their feelings and needs as you're trying to grow your business with their help. It is important that you have your finger on their pulse so that you can tell whether they're comfortable or not. If they're comfortable, things will work out for you in many ways. For one, they're going to push your brand. For another, you're possibly going to develop a very good friendship.

☐ 203   OVERNIGHT

I have had many people come to me with an idea and state that the reason it's such a good idea is that there's nothing like it out there. "It so good that it's going to be a hit very quickly. It's going to be an overnight success." This is not a good reason to start a business.

The number one reason to start a business is because you have a passion for it. The second reason to start a business is because there's a market for it. The third reason is because you hate, with all of your might, with the very fiber of your being, having a boss. Three reasons.

There are no overnight successes. Stop acting like it.

☐ 204   DONE > PERFECT

Recently, I was told that I should take my time and make sure I do it right. For the most part, that's right. You should definitely take your time and make sure you do things right and plan things out. But being done is always going to be better than being perfect. If you're worried about how perfect you're going to get it, you probably won't start. Lewis & Clark are known because they were pioneers of the Northwest. On their way out, as with all pioneers, they didn't push through and pave a road behind them. They just pushed through enough to set the course and make a trail so that others could come after them and make a cleaner, more perfect version of their venture out West. In a lot of ways, that's how entrepreneurs are. The best entrepreneurs are the pioneers. They don't necessarily make a clean, paved road behind them. Usually, it's a mess behind them but they push forward. Entrepreneurship is messy. It always has been. It always will be dirty.

☐ 205   STRUGGLE

I've met to a lot of entrepreneurs who talked about struggle after struggle after struggle. That's the way entrepreneurship is. It is the way it is. We are on the frontlines. We're the warriors. We're the roughnecks. We're the ones in the trenches, smoking a cigarette, bleeding from multiple parts of our body. Hoping we get to see our kids again.

If you're thinking about being an entrepreneur and starting your own company, know that it's going to be a daily grind. A daily effort. Getting up and putting one foot in front of the other, and making it happen. Pushing through and being tenacious. If you don't think you have it, then maybe you don't. I guess that's what separates us all. If you're thinking, "Man, I don't know if I can handle it," then possibly, most likely, or definitely, you're not going to be able to handle it.

To all you entrepreneurs out there, keep getting up. We're all going through it. Do the grind, go to work, grind it out, come home, take a break. But do it again and again. For all of you thinking about it: We don't need any more workers in the middle. Do it! Start today.

☐ 206 WHY NOT

Sometimes I think my job is to talk people *out* of starting a company, and sometimes I think it's to talk people *into* starting a company. I had a meeting with a person who was asking me about entrepreneurship, what it takes, what I thought of his concepts, and I found myself talking him out of starting his own company. It was weird for me because I'm usually talking people into starting companies, but I feel that if I can talk you *out* of starting a company, then you probably shouldn't start one.

Top Three Reasons NOT to Start a Company

1. You're the last to get paid.

2. All liability falls on you.

Your company dangles on a string that can be severed at any moment by the government, a lawsuit, or an employee. It's super risky.

3. Heavy is the head that wears the crown

Last night I came home, my wife said, "Man, there's something...something off about you." We talked and worked through it and finally, we agreed that there was nothing that we could put our finger on except that there is a lot of pressure on the business owner. There are a lot of eyes and a lot of people that depend on you to deliver in your area as a business owner. That can wear you out very quickly.

If I haven't talked you out of starting your own business, go do it right now. It is totally worth it.

☐ 207 SHAWSHANK

Sales can be hard. Phone calls, emails, tracking where you are in several conversations, making people feel wanted, appreciated, and liked. There are so many plates spinning in sales.

Remember the movie Shawshank Redemption? That was such a good movie. Remember how Andy escaped? All he did was take his little rock hammer and picked his way through his cell wall until he broke through into his freedom. After he got through the wall there was a lot of shit he had to crawl through, but he was victorious in escaping prison.

That's what sales is like. Just a little poking through, dealing with the same thing every day, finding that one sweet spot that you're picking at every day until one day you break through. There's lots of crap you've got to endure once you're through, but you get through. In sales, you have a fixed position. Everybody knows where you're coming from. Word of mouth starts to spread. It all starts with just poking through, just trying that little bit.

Are you picking at that one spot, trying to break through? Have you already done it? If you have, high five! If you're haven't, keep working at it. Let's break out of your Shawshank of sales.

☐ 208 THANKS

If you thank your customers, they'll come back. I'm amazed at the amount of businesses I walk into that don't thank their customers.

Appreciation station—set one up. I don't care what it looks like, there needs to be an element of your company that is thanking your customers, so that they'll come back.

☐ 209 SHOW'EM

November 1955. A young man is about to get into his car in the town of Hill Valley. He sees that there's an older gentleman there in the driver's seat. He says, "Get in. We're related." The guy gets into the car. The older gentleman drives him to his house. When they get inside the house, the older gentlemen hands him a book. The Gray's Sports Almanac. He hands it to the guy and he says, "Here in this book are listings of all the sports games winnings over the next few decades. If you were to bet on those numbers, you would be rich." The younger gentleman eventually throws the Gray's Sports Almanac into the back, to which the older gentlemen grabs it and hits him over the head.

He says, "You idiot. You can make a fortune on this!" The younger gentleman doesn't get it. The older gentleman turns on the radio to the sports channel to the end of a baseball game. The old man predicts that there's going to be an upset. The younger gentlemen states, "That's ridiculous!" Alas, there was an upset. Then the younger gentleman gets it. That's when he sees the value of this Gray's Sports Almanac. He didn't understand it until he saw it actually happen.

What are you selling? Are you showing it to people or are you telling them about it? If you've got a product, it's pretty easy. You just show it to him. But if you're selling a service, are you just telling them about it or are you showing it to them? They're not going to get it unless you do. Sounds like an easy question to answer, but it's not. Take your service, put it to use right in front of your potential client. It'll work. It's important that they see it happen.

☐ 210   TEA

I like a good tea. Hot tea, cold tea, sweet tea, green tea. Getting the best tea out of your teabag is an art. John Lennon swore that the tea bag must go into the cup and then you must pour the water so it hits the tea bag and that's how the tea gets out. If I'm making a good hot tea, I put the bag in there for five minutes and pull it right out when time's up. If I happen to forget about it and I leave it in there, the tea gets a little bitter. It's ruined.

Let's talk about staying in the cup a little too long. A gentleman came to me to talk about his business. He told me that he was bored. He had some questions about how to sell a business. We talked for a while and I gave him some input. One of the things I left him with was that if you stay in your business for too long, you're going to ruin it.

Some entrepreneurs can get into a company, stay in it their whole lives, grow their legacy, and love it. Some entrepreneurs are just good starters. We lose sleep, we grind, we make connections, we put it all together, but we make no money. We love it. Then all of a sudden the business starts working and making money. Policies and procedures get put into place and it goes into cruise control…and we become bored. It's at that point that we need to pull the tea bag out. You know why? We can make the company bitter. If we've done it right the staff around us knows how to run our business way better than we do. The more we show up and the more we get our hands in there after the building process, the more we can make it bitter.

Have you stayed in your business for too long? Is it stagnant because of you? Are you afraid to move on and start another venture because the rules say you're only allowed to start one company at a time? I did some checking—that's not the rule. Maybe you need to sell the company. Maybe you need to let the staff run it. Maybe it's time for you to take yourself out of the equation. Don't ruin the tea.

☐ 211 OUTSTAND

Hood to Coast—where you run from Mt. Hood to the coast of Oregon. It's 199 miles. But you don't do it by yourself. You do it with a big team. Each member has to run 12 miles of that, but it still is a long run. I know for a fact that I am not the fastest person on our team, and our team is not going to be the fastest one to complete the relay in large part because of me, but I know that we'll finish, and I know that I'll complete my 12 miles because that's what's important.

In the same sense, that's what business is like. The best business owners and the most successful entrepreneurs are not the fastest. They're not the smartest. They're not the best workers. They're not the best people to be around. They're not the strongest. But they are always the last person standing.

That's how I know I will succeed in business. I am not the smartest or most efficient. I'm not the best person to be around. But I am really good at being the last person standing. I can just outstand you.

Are you still standing? Are you still trying? Do you keep going? Make sure that you are getting up and going to work and doing work, and you'll win.

☐ 212 GLENGARRY

Have you ever seen the movie Glengarry Glen Ross? If you haven't, you need to watch it, because it's Jack Lemmon at his best. It's an amazing movie. It's really underrated, but if you're in sales or if you sell anything, you definitely need to see this movie. These guys portray the role of salesmen; dirty, sleazy, just salesman-y salesmen. You just feel so bad for the people these guys are selling to and you feel bad for these salesmen and their lives. It's terrible. It's a great movie but for terrible reasons.

Salesmen get the worst reputation. Maybe because it comes from people doing really bad sales jobs or manipulating customers, but the fact is that **people buy things**. You have to buy stuff. You buy stuff every day. Therefore people have to sell stuff, so there have to be salesmen in this world. If you are selling something, if you are in sales, put yourself in the shoes of the person you're selling to. The worst thing you could do is be motivated by moving the product at any cost. That's how salesmen get a bad reputation. People selling things for the fact that they want to sell things.

Just put yourself in a spot whereby when they're ready to need it, you're there. Not knocking on the door all the time, not sending emails and phone calls all the time. Just stay right inside that line where you're just like, "Oh yeah, I remember Chip talking about Perkbird. Maybe I will give that a try." If you're jamming it down peoples throat, it's just going to come back. It's going to be bad. Even if they use it, it's going to be bad.

☐ 213   FEELING

I love massages. I didn't know how good they were until I finally let somebody give me a massage. I get them all the time now, professional massages. You get in there, you get naked, you lay on the table, and they have nice music playing. I say to the masseuse, "I don't know what you're doing, but I think massages help me because you're pushing the bad blood out of my muscles so good blood can go in." She says, "You're completely wrong, that's not what's happening, but if that's what gets you in here, then good."

That's how things are sometimes with my daily work schedule. Sometimes, in the back of my head, when I have a very busy day and I think I did a lot of work and feel accomplished, I wonder if I really am accomplished. Did I really accomplish stuff or was I doing things that didn't matter and don't move me forward?

Do you ever think that way too? I'm here to abolish that thought. All work is good. Maybe you are efficient, maybe you're not, but I know that if you go to work and put some time into whatever you're working on, it's always good. Sometimes, it's that feeling that keeps us going. Sometimes, that feeling is all we need. That feeling's important. Make sure you feel the feeling. Let that guide you.

☐ 214   MEET

Do you love football? I love football. There's nothing more American than football. Football is a serious sport, there's millions and billions of dollars on the line. We must get it right. We must work together as a team so that we can win the Super Bowl. We all make lots of money, we all suck in a bunch of confetti, we bring our kids up on stage, lick the trophy. We have a great time.

Football players don't show up on the first day, jump on the field, and start bashing each other up. They meet, they plot, they plan. They figure out who's best for where. Everybody's input is put together, chewed up, mashed in, produced into something solid. Is your company doing that? Are you getting together?

I'm amazed that so many of the small businesses I deal with don't have a staff meeting. They don't come together. There might be a memo, a company email, mass text, or Slack, but they don't come together. This is a business; this is somebody's, if not a lot of body's, livelihood.

"Chip, it's too expensive to get everybody together on one day. I have to pay for everybody to be here."

You're going to pay for everybody to leave your company if you don't come together. Have a meeting at least once a month, all hands on deck, talk, spit out ideas, chew them up, mash them together, produce something solid.

☐ 215   SINNOVATION

"*...And if it ain't broken then don't try to fix it. And think of the summers of the past. Adjust the base and let the alpine blast.*" If it ain't broke then don't try to fix it. That's the first time I heard that phrase. Will Smith and DJ Jazzy Jeff. Summertime.

If it's not broken, don't try to fix it. You are sinning sometimes by innovating. Sinnovation. So many times we innovate for the sake of innovating. No. Innovation needs to come when it's time to recreate.

There are parts of your company that you want to always be innovating in. Trying out new things. Innovate. Innovate. Innovate. But there are other parts of the company that are working. They're your cash cow. Don't change them. Ride it until the wheels fall off. Don't innovate around your cash cow, your flagship, your main means of income. That would be sinnovation. It's a sin to innovate on something that is working. Innovation for the sake of innovation is a no-go.

Innovate to test the market. Innovate to test your crew. Innovate to test an idea. Test. Test. Test. Don't innovate on something that's working. That's the quickest way to break it.

☐ 216   CLICK

Marriage is hard. My wife is a marriage and family therapist. She said to me that there is this phenomenon where couples can go from feeling that it's completely over to good—just like that.

Business is hard, and just like marriage, when you think it's over, something clicks, and you're back to good. If you're at that place, just take one more step, do one more a day, do one more hour, do one more minute, do one more second. Give it that next bit.

Who knows, it might just let up a little. It might just click, and all make sense, and you'll be back to good.

☐ 217   SALSA

Remember the last time you had a big tomato and just bit into it? Remember the last time you got that onion, this really good onion, and just ate it? No? Do you remember the last time you squeezed some lime juice into a cup, and just chugged it down? Remember? No? What about the last time you just got some cilantro, just gnawed it? Or you took cumin seasoning and dumped it down your throat? No! You don't remember. Nobody does that. Maybe the tomato, but nobody does that. If you took all those ingredients, chopped them up, put them together, you get a fine salsa. Those things individually, meh. YUCK!

As entrepreneurs, we have a tendency to not want any input. We have a tendency to say, "My way or the highway." Run the ship as the captain and the dictator. To be successful, you need all the ingredients mixed together. You need a lot of things put together. You need a lot of people involved helping you make decisions. You're still the king. You're still the leader. They'll all respect you, but you have to let people's voices be heard. You have to take your ideas to the people that help you run your company. Businesses can't be run as a dictatorship. You need input. To get really good ideas you have to pull everybody's minds together. My way or the highway doesn't last very long. It doesn't make for good companies.

Get everybody's heads together. Work through these ideas. Let people object. Let people push back. You'll refine your idea and everybody will love you for it.

☐ 218   TEQUILA

Remember your first tequila night? Oh buddy, so not good. Had a little beer then you had a little liquor. Not good for the palate. Liquor before beer, you're in the clear. Beer before liquor, never been sicker. Customer before company you're in the clear. Company before customer, never been sicker.

There are moments in life as an entrepreneur where you have to decide between what's best for your customers and what's best for your company. Customers should always win over company because without the customers you don't have a company. The moment you put your company first and customers second is the moment your company will start to die. Seek ye first the customer. Second, the company.

So many of us as entrepreneurs are tempted to play the short game. Deciding what's best for the company over the customer is very short game-minded. Are the decisions you're making, when it comes to customer and company, long or short-game decisions? In the long run happy customers means a healthy company. Happy customers, healthy company. Healthy company, happy employees. Happy employees, better community. Better community, better customers. CIRCLE OF LIFE.

☐ 219 STAND OUT

I remember when we used to take peroxide and put it in our hair. Maybe it looked cool because it was white, but then when it grew out, it looked like we had frosted tips. I just wanted to look like Flea from the Red Hot Chili Peppers. It was great. I went brunette and then I put my initials in there. I did so many things because I wanted to stand out.

You have to stand out to get what you want. A buddy of mine asked me, "When I'm hiring, what is it that I should look for?" The answer is always the same. It's not what you've done. That's important, but it's not everything. It's not how smart you are. It's not which school you went to. It's not how many jobs you had and where. It's not the people you know. It's your work ethic.

I worked for a company and I was brand new. We had just gone through an employee overhaul, and we needed to do a mass hire. I put out an ad. It was a come-one, come-all cattle call, two solid days of 30-minute interviews. At the end of each interview, I would say, "Thank you. The interview went well. If we're interested, we'll call you. Do not call us back." We took their résumés, threw them into a drawer and shut it, and waited for the phone to ring. The people who called me back and gave the extra effort were the ones whom I gave a second interview to. I can confidently say that they were the hardest working and most talented people I interviewed.

If you want to stand out, kids, people, everybody in transition looking to stand out, here's how you do it: Work hard. Show good work ethic. By just doing that one thing, you'll stand out among the rest. I will take work ethic over education, connections, or experience any day.

☐ 220   HAPPY

Sometimes I get really into hobbies that take my mind off work because it then helps me work better (refer to Lesson 197 "PLAY"). Recently, I got into baking bread. Whoa, so much fun. Take flour, water, egg, salt, and mix it all together, then mix it with yeast, and let it sit. It rises, you push it down and it rises again. So much fun. Then I found out that you can make sourdough bread by using wild yeast. So you're literally making bread with two ingredients. Now we're talking pure food. Healthy food. So I studied up on how to do it, and here's how: Put a little bit of flour in a bowl. Add water. Mix until it's nice and pasty and then you let it sit. First day, nothing. Second day, a little bubbly. Third day, lots of bubbles. By the fourth day, this bowl of yeast has taken off. Going crazy. Wild little yeast in there just eating themselves and eating everything else, making bacteria, eating bacteria, and causing this live bowl of yeast. Then you take that and mix it in with your bread mixture. You have wild yeast and you can make your own sourdough bread. It only took a little bit to get it started.

The other day my chiropractor asked, "How are you doing?"

"Man, I am so happy."

"That's terrific. You're always happy. It must take a lot of work to be that happy."

"Nope, only in the beginning. It only takes a little bit of work of being positive and staying happy, until it starts to grow on itself."

Are there bad days? Yes. Things happen, absolutely. Is this world terrible? Absolutely not. Do you want to be happy, stay positive, and have that energy affect your business and the people around you? It just takes a little bit of effort in the beginning and then watch it just grow and grow and grow. Pretty soon, before you know it, you're happy. And you'll get to stay that way without much further effort.

☐ 221   OCEAN

Now that my kids are getting older, I'm really excited to teach them how to surf. One of the things I always tell people learning how to surf is not to fight the ocean. The ocean is way bigger than you, but it's also a lot slower and dumber. Don't try and fight it, just be faster than it. Relax when it's winning, but fight when it turns its back on you. Outsmart the ocean.

It's the same way with us, entrepreneurs, and starting up companies that are small. Often, our competitors are bigger than us. They're stronger than us, but don't be turned off. Don't give up, because you're faster and probably smarter than they are.

☐ 222   RUN

I watched the Olympic marathon event last summer. There was an American runner from Oregon State University who got the bronze medal. It was amazing. It was the first time in years that an American was in the top three. At his interview, they asked:

"How'd you like the race?"

"You know, for marathons not being my focus, I think I did pretty well. I might switch to being a marathon runner."

Sometimes we're good at something we are not focusing on. That athlete knew he was good at running, but he discovered he was also good at running marathons.

Sometimes as business owners, we can be focusing on something we're not so good at, when in fact, what we are good at is just around the corner. Whatever you're spending time on—is that something you're most skilled in?

☐ 223   FRUIT

You know what I love about Oregon? Food grows everywhere. Everywhere you go during the summer there are apples, grapes, blackberries, marion berries, strawberries, etc., etc.. The other day, the kids and I were out walking through a park when we came across two berry bushes. One was growing amazing fruit. The other was growing really bad berries. They were right next to each other. I couldn't figure out why they were so different. I started looking around the base of the second bush and saw that it was growing sideways on a rock and not able to really get into the ground. Its branches were frail. The other berry bush was fine, it had plenty of ground to grow on.

All of us in sales and business development have to be good at networking. You have to give, give, give, receive, give, give, give, receive. That's all networking is—connecting, listening, seeing, listening, seeing, listening, seeing. While networking you might come across some crusty bushes and limbs that are growing out of a rock. Sometimes it can be tempting to look for fruit from those unfortunate bushes. Crusty limbs never lead to good fruit. If you find a crusty limb, snip it off and walk away. Sometimes you'll be tempted, "I know this guy, and this guy knows this girl, and this girl could lead to this girl, and that could be a big sale." That's never going to happen from a crusty limb or bush. It's always going to produce really bad fruit.

Look for the bush that grows from the ground—it'll bear the sweetest fruit.

☐ 224   BEACH

I love the beach. I like sitting out there all day, having a good time. I like getting in the water, eating peanut butter and jelly sandwiches, getting sand in my feet, my armpits, and my mouth. It's so much fun. My daughter likes going to the beach too. However, she doesn't like the same beach activities as I do. Same adventure, different experience. My daughter doesn't like to get sandy. She doesn't like to go into the water. She doesn't like sand in her food. She doesn't like to be there for very long. Same activity, different experience.

In the same way, we entrepreneurs can get sidetracked by thinking that our customers like the same things we do about our product or service. We often think that the experience of doing business with us is the same experience for every customer, but it's not. It's a different experience for everyone. We can't assume that our reaction will be the same as our customers.

I have a friend who sells carpet. Our relationship started back when I bought blue carpet from him. He wrapped it up, shipped it over, and had his guys bring it to my office. When it got there, I didn't think they had delivered the right color. His carpet installers thought otherwise. So my friend rushed over. He didn't argue whether it was blue carpet or not. It wasn't blue to me, his customer, therefore it wasn't blue to him. He didn't try to talk me into the fact that it might be blue carpet. He told his guys to wrap it up and get it out of there so that he could get me the carpet that I wanted.

It's not what we think our customers are getting—it's what our *customers* think they are getting. Try that tweak in your business.

☐ 225   WORK

When I was a kid, some of the most influential people in my life were the leaders around me. These were the pastors, business owners, authors, and speakers, among others. Every time they sat me down and gave me advice, I listened. So I'm going to do something here—

To those of you who have kids, 10 to 17 years old, go get them right now. Force them to listen to you reading this out loud. I'll give you a second.

Alright. Are they there?

Hi. Welcome. You're amazing. I'm in awe of the amazing things you're going to do in your life. I'm proud of you and excited for you. I want to say another thing. If you don't work hard in life, you will not get the things that you want, ever. Here it is again. If you don't work hard in life, you will not get the things that you want, ever. Alright. You may go, now.

To you, parents, leaders, everyone else reading: Work ethic is taught at a very young age. Get on it. I am hearing from the small business owners in your community that they cannot find people who are willing to work. It starts with you, not the young people.

☐ 226   TIME

I just ran a really long race. It felt like this:

Relay races are tough! You're in a van for 30 hours. You run for three of those hours. The rest of the time, you're trying to get your body back in order to run again. You're on no sleep and your body's starting to lie to you. It's telling you that you're not hungry or thirsty, when you really are. Your body starts playing tricks on you and you have to do all these things to keep it ready for your next leg. You're eating electrolytes. You're woofing down protein, sugar, and carbohydrates. You're drinking weird sauces and putting on weird salves.

As a consultant to small business owners, sometimes I wish there was a salve that I could give to my clients. You'd open it up and rub it on whatever area is ailing you. That salve would be called "Time". I often tell my clients, "Just give it a little more time. Just rub some time on it." As entrepreneurs, we have a tendency to get impatient. We don't want to wait any longer. We don't want to work another day. We don't want to have another conversation. We don't want another phone call or another email. We just want this success behind us and headed off towards our next success.

Sometimes, to get to that first success you have to rub a little salve on it. Take some business electrolytes. You need that certain something that's going to give you a little bit more endurance because it truly is time that heals all wounds and also leads to success. Patience is a virtue, and I wish it was a salve.

☐ 227 RISK

Managing risks in business is a lot like fishing.

I used to fish a lot. The funny thing about fishing is that you don't always catch a fish. You can study the weather, get the temperature of the water, have the best bait and best lure, slow roll it, and pick and chew it, but you still might not catch any fish.

In business, you can test the market, do analysis, get the only dot com there is for that word, run it by your lucky uncle, rub a rabbit's foot on it, but that's still not going to tell you if it's going to work. There are businesses that tested horribly. They weren't supposed to work but they work fine and made billions of dollars. There were businesses where all the signs pointed to success but they didn't work one lick.

In the end, you just have to decide whether to do it or not. How do I manage risks? I take it. I take risks. Sometimes it works out, sometimes it doesn't. If that scares you, you're probably not an entrepreneur and that's fine because most of the world is not built for that.

☐ 228   DOUBLE

Three Things You Can Implement Into Your Business That Will Help You Scale

1. Don't change status

Make sure you are not changing status. You own your business. Make sure that that stays. Don't become an employee of somebody else's business hoping to scale yours. That's the opposite direction. Sounds funny, but people do it. They get sucked into it. Don't do it.

2. Get rid of things you don't do best

You might do them well, but you don't do it the best. Sub that stuff out. It's still your work, just find somebody to do it for you and turn it in. Let somebody else do your homework.

3. Double your price

Sounds counter-intuitive, counterproductive, opposite, backwards. Sounds like what you don't want to do, but it is what you want to do. One day, while touring the US, somebody pulled me aside and said:

"I'm going to challenge you to double your fee."

"What, like work up to more over the next couple months?"

"No. Overnight, double your fee. The next person that calls and asks what your fee is for doing improv comedy, take what you normally charge and double it."

I thought he was crazy, but I did it, and from that day on, we doubled our fee. Then the next year, we doubled that. Doubling your price sets expectations in a different place (I'm not going to say higher expectations, because you're already delivering). It causes the person who's hiring you to treat you better. We started getting waters before our show, limos were picking us up from the airport, crowds were bigger and better because we assumed a higher value, and then we delivered.

☐ 229   BAND

Today at my co-working space I listened to two people form a band. So and so found out he could play the guitar. It was awesome. I found myself asking, "Why does he want to be in a band? There's other fun stuff to do." Then I thought, oh yeah, I've been in a band. It was so much fun. Why are they fun? There's something about doing something together.

I think that's what I like about running a business. You have all these moving parts and the outcome is this one thing—a business. The thrill of it is trying to get everybody to work in unison and be efficient. Having the same output. Rocking at the same time.

Are you enjoying it? Get together and make businesses. And have fun doing it.

☐ 230   HEART

My wife always tells me that I am a very black-and-white person. There are not very many times when I fall into the gray area, and while this doesn't work so well in marriage, it works terrific in business. In entrepreneurship and small business, you need to make decisions from your gut. What's your instinct telling you? Businesses exist to make a profit, so when you start making decisions from your heart, not your head, you're going to get mixed up.

For example, I see clients hiring people because they feel sorry for them. HR is not a place for the altruistic side of you to come out. While I'm not encouraging you to be heartless, make your decisions from your head and not your heart. Start a non-profit if you'd like to help people out. Have a portion of your profit put away for you to give back to your community and the people you believe in. But hiring somebody just to help them out is not good motivation and probably will lead to that position being filled by somebody who lacks the skills and ability to perform.

☐ 231   MOVIES

Movie theaters are one of my very favorite business models. You'd think the majority of the profit would be made from movies, but it's not. The majority of the money comes from concessions, but it's not called a concession theater, which is what it should be named. Movies are merely the commercials to get you there to spend money on snacks and drinks. A movie theater without concessions would go under very quickly.

Maybe your business makes most of its profit from what it's named after, but what are some areas that you can add an attraction to bring more business to you, outside of advertising?

☐ 232   KAP

My kids play outside in our neighborhood a lot. We always have so much fun, but our neighborhood is getting bigger and therefore, experiencing a lot more traffic. I am worried about my children getting hit by a car in front of my house, so what did I do? I bought a sign. It's one of those signs with kids and flags. It's supposed to warn everybody that there are kids at play. Who looks at those? Everybody. Who stops and slows down because of them? Nobody. I threw that sign away. I went into my garage and pulled out an old sign that somebody gave me from advertising guitar lessons. It's a frame that sits out there in the middle of the road. Everybody stops. They want to read the sign. It looks different. It's very effective.

People have seen the Kid At Play sign a million times, with the flag sticking out and all its reflectors. They are blinded to it because they've seen it a lot. Now guitar lessons, however…Heck next week I might give away a free turtle. I'm going to frequently change the message on that sign so that drivers don't get desensitized to it.

What are you doing in advertising right now that people are blinded to? What are they seeing all the time? *Hey, buy my thing. Hey, come to my thing. Look at my Instagram and Facebook post.* They're getting blinded. Change it up a little bit. Make people stop and look at what you're advertising. If you don't, hypothetically your kids are in danger.

☐ 233   IPHONE

Have you seen the new iPhone? I cannot wait to get that thing. I'm excited about this new one coming out. The camera is so sophisticated that I have friends in the photography industry who are speechless. I work with one on almost a daily basis. We were talking about how the new iPhone camera can shoot pictures as good as he can with a real camera. He isn't worried about his business, though, because he's smart. That's just one percent of the reason why he is not afraid of innovation, because all the value of his service is placed squarely on him. He is the proprietary part of his business. He's the secret sauce. Without him a good camera is just a good camera.

All good business people do this. They make themselves the proprietary part of their business. No one can tell a story like he can, put it together like he can, get the angle that he wants, and edit the way he can. He tells stories with visuals. He doesn't just take good pictures. He said, "I could go out and buy the best stove in the world. The best oven, the best kitchen appliance, but it doesn't make me a good cook."

Are you making yourself the proprietary part of your business?

There's a caveat to this. If you plan on exiting and selling your business, you have to start weaning yourself out of that position (see Lesson 172 "S&Ps"). If you're not, or are not even thinking about it, then you have to put yourself in a position where you are the crucial aspect to the product or service that you're putting out.

☐ 234   JET SKI

One of my high school jobs was renting out jet skis on Madera Beach, Florida. I would stand in waist-high water at the beach and talk to tourists for eight hours a day. SO. MUCH. FUN. It was also very hot so I drank a lot of fluids, which meant I had to go to the bathroom a lot. Since I was standing in a big ocean I'd just *let it go* (only for number one, come on people). After a couple months, since I was in such a habit of just letting it go, I'd have to consciously make a decision to not go when in public. There would be times where I was with friends at night and think, "Oh wait, I can't go right now, I'm not in waist-high water."

It's funny, the human brain. Used, dealt with, worked, trained, and disciplined, the brain can be an amazing tool but left on its own…If you don't pressure yourself and just let yourself go, the brain can turn on you.

Train your brain. Don't just let it do its thing. Be intentional about training the brain. Get a discipline. Have something you dedicate it to everyday. Push it to focus often. Get uncomfortable.

☐ 235   TOGETHER

I watched a special about how people used to think the atom was the smallest particle. Then they figured out how to split an atom into smaller particles, and they split those particles further down to one little tiny, mini particle. They found that these little, tiny particles want to join together. When they join together they make an atom, and when an atom joins together with other atoms it makes a molecule, and then molecules make cells. Life in our solar system is trying to compound itself and build each other. They want to come together. Humans were built to come together.

It gets lonely running a business. People around you don't understand what you're going through. Maybe they turn their back on you because of how much time you spend working. There is just not enough of you to go around and that turns people away. All of a sudden you find that it's just you. Just one person doing everything. I want to let you know that that's completely normal. That happens to everyone. I also want to encourage you to work hard, be dedicated, and stay focused. Keep that goal in mind, be consistent, but take time to come together with other entrepreneurs. They're lonely, too. Spend extra time bringing others like us together in certain ways, like joining a co-working space, meet-up group, calling on the phone—reach out to other entrepreneurs.

Entrepreneurship is very lonely but it doesn't have to be. It just takes that little bit of a push so that one little entrepreneur can connect with the next entrepreneur, and the next, and the next, and the next, so we can come together. We're made to.

☐ 236   KID

As a parent, one thing I've figured out is that kids perform better with structure. They feel more comfortable. They might not like you for doing it but in the end they'll be really glad that they had that structure.

An entrepreneur is a lot like a kid without rules or limits. We could just take the day off whenever we decide to. Are we tired of working? We could stop working. Is the surf up? Is the weather great? We can just check right out. When you don't have somebody setting your schedule, or making sure you're clocked in and are productive, it can be hard to keep your pulse on whether you're making efficient decisions or not.

Oftentimes I encourage my clients and other entrepreneurs to set limits. "I'm going to put in 40 hours a week." Put it in the schedule. Make sure you get those 40 hours a week in. Now, you might have to take time to let your brain reset. You really do need to set some parameters on how you are going to work, because if you don't, you're just going to be that kid in the pit throwing balls at people and whining.

☐ 237   KODAK

I had to bring my car to the auto repair shop. I busted a radiator hose. The auto shop was in the same building as a cab company. While I was waiting for my car to get fixed, I started noticing a theme. It seemed like the cab company was really mad at Uber. There was a decal of a kid urinating on an Uber logo. "F Uber" was written everywhere. I tried to put myself in both the cab company and Uber's shoes. If I owned a cab company, my reaction would not be to hate Uber. It would be to outsmart Uber. Saying you hate your competition is the equivalent of a kid who throws himself to the floor and starts beating the ground.

For instance, look at Kodak, a leader in film processing and cameras. Kodak was living the dream. Then the industry started to tweak a little bit. Everything was going digital. You can take pictures from this thing you call a phone. The internet got bigger. There was no reason to really print anything or use film. Did Kodak throw themselves to the floor and start wailing and beating the ground, screaming things? Maybe, but I know what happened in public was that they simply pivoted. They outsmarted where the industry was going. They hopped out of line, ran straight up to the beginning and jumped back in line. Today, if you look at Kodak, they're killing it. They just changed the nature of their association with their customers.

It appears that we have to change the nature of our association. Who's beating you and can you hop out of line and go up and get in front of them? Get off the ground, stop whining, and use your head to get in front of your competitors.

☐ 238   MEDALS

Racing is interesting. In my last race, there were times that were happy and fun and there were times that really sucked. Mostly, it was just so long and arduous that that feeling when you crossed the finish line was such a rush. It took us about 30 hours to do it. We did not beat anybody or break any records, but what we did do was finish, and for that, they gave us a medal and that's all I was hoping for.

A day doesn't go by where I'm not reminded that the secret to running a small business is just putting in the work. Small business is an endurance sport and everybody who doesn't give up, doesn't stop, and keeps going, WINS.

Keep going, you small business owners. That's all you have to do. You don't have to run, you don't have to walk, you don't have to crawl, just keep moving forward.

☐ 239   CONNECTOR

Surrounding yourself with good, positive people is great on its own, but it also helps great people connect with other great people. It's just as good for you as it is for them. You've seen these people. They're connectors. They know. Do you know what they do the best that other people don't? They listen, they remember. Listening and remembering will make you a good connector.

Listen. Remember. See if you can't connect somebody to someone else whom you have nothing to gain from.

☐ 240   BRAVE

One of my favorite spots to surf is deep into the Baja Peninsula of Mexico. It's always really fun, but it is really hard to get out past the shore break. You also have the Mexican police to deal with. I have made several trips there with friends, particularly, my friend Chad. Chad is the type of person who makes you feel safe, no matter where you're going or what you're doing. He just has that sense about him. For instance, if something was going wrong—if we were getting jumped by somebody or if our car broke down—Chad was going to be able to handle it. It was Chad's sense of leadership that really made it okay to go into dangerous territory. To this day, Chad has that effect.

What kind of leader are you in your company? Do the people you lead have the same feelings? Do they feel like, "Hey if stuff goes down, Chip's going to handle it"? Do they feel safe when they're around you? Do they feel safe in knowing that maybe you're not the strongest or the smartest, but you're definitely the bravest? The best business leaders are brave. They're calm under pressure. They might not always feel that way, but it always seems that way.

Are you a brave leader? Will your people follow you into battle? Follow you into danger? Do they feel safe with you around? If not, let's get there. You and your team will benefit from it greatly.

☐ 241   DRIVE

Drive. Where does it come from?

While watching football one weekend, one of my buddies said, "Do you realize that when you watch professional football, you're looking at the top .000001 percent of athletes in this world performing at their highest level? They are the most talented, gifted, and driven athletes."

Drive, where does it come from? Are we born with it? Do we find it when we find our passion? Do our parents or guardians instill it in us?

I think drive comes from something you want intensely. For some people it's money, achievements, happiness, or joy. Are you driven right now? Is your focus on one of those things I just mentioned? Or are you finding yourself very un-driven, unmotivated? If you are, it could be that your focus is off.

Where's your focus? Is it something that gives you passion and that gives you drive? Or somewhere along the way, have you lost sight of what it is that you're going at? What are you going at?

☐ 242   DIGITAL

Here's some quick advice for those of you who have business ideas:

If you really want to start a company, spend a good amount of time thinking about a digital company, something online, harnessing technology. That way, you have a less expensive option for getting proof of concept.

☐ 243   WORK

You might have good work ethic if:

1. You had a really challenging childhood, where you were left with no choice but to work. You do it for yourself. You get yourself up and do it.

2. You had terrific parents who taught you that the key to life is to work hard, and that there's no room for whining or complaining. There's no room for laziness or things that are half-assed done.

3. As an adult, you had a massive change of life event—things were going one way, then something happened, and you completely flipped it and started going another way.

If you have work ethic, which one are you? If you don't have work ethic, how are you going to find it?

☐ 244   PAPER

I go to coffee shops when I have time to kill between meetings. There was one time that I was sitting next to a lady who looked like she was studying lines? Writing a paper? I don't know what she was doing, but she had a lot of paper. As she got up, one piece of paper flew away. 50 miles/hour wind. Crazy. In my mind, there was no way she would get it back. But she surprised me.

She threw the rest of her papers under her book bag and took off. (Of course I'm watching her because this is pretty freakin' entertaining.) She went over a curb across the street. She hopped over bushes, went through the bushes, under a car...She was halfway across the parking lot when she scooped up that one piece of paper. It was pretty impressive. As she came back, I said, "You know, I didn't have much faith in you, but you did it. You caught that paper." Then she said something enlightening: "Yeah. I just had to get ahead of it." Solid response, lady at the coffee shop.

What is it that you need to get ahead of? This challenge is for myself too. I'm not good at this. I'm a here-and-now type of guy. I know how to do "now". I don't know how to do "ahead" very well.

There are some things you (and I) need to get ahead of. Highlight those things today. We'll catch that paper.

☐ 245   MARATHON

I've said this before—business is a marathon, not a sprint. My comedy club was just like any other another business. We put on multiple shows a week. When we had low attendance, it didn't change our effort. We would perform to three people the same way we would to 1000. (If we had three people per show for six months, there would have been a different issue to address.)

All sales people, entrepreneurs, and baseball players go through slumps. You have to just keep getting in that batters box and swing that bat.

The success of your business will be measured by the sum of all your days, not the few that you wish didn't happen.

☐ 246   NECTAR

The largest deciding factor between an entrepreneur and a non-entrepreneur is your ability to take risks. If you're easily deterred by competition, money, or security, then starting a company isn't for you.

I had somebody tell me this week that they weren't going to start a company because they were the first person to start that kind of company in their city. Competition is what keeps entrepreneurs up at night. It's what wakes us up early in the morning. It is half of the game. It is the invention of the game. We start companies to be better than other companies that are like the ones we're starting.

It seems like our country has created this culture of being safe—although we are aware of the rewards you can reap from taking risks, we're still not willing to take it. We don't want to taste the sweetest nectar. We're okay with the COSTCO brand nectar. We don't want the homegrown, local, nectar. If you think you can handle risk, I urge you to follow the path towards that sweet, homegrown, local nectar of self-employment.

☐ 247   PRODUCTIVITY

Take breaks and reward yourself throughout the day. This will help your productivity. If you reach a milestone in your day, take a break. Do something fun that takes your mind off things. You're helping your brain reset and start being efficient again. Often, during those breaks are when you come up with your breakthroughs. Take breaks for breakthroughs.

☐ 248   UNDER-FIRE

I was an entrepreneur before I even knew it. I was thrown into the fire and found out that that's where I performed best, under fire. I was helping my church run a coffee house and doing comedy. I started doing comedy outside the coffee house, at which point they kicked me out of the church. I decided to do more comedy and had to make it happen by booking shows. I had no other option. The pressure was on. After a few years I realized that I had started my first company and was making my living working for myself. It wasn't a terribly good living, but I was seeing the world and had money in my pocket. For me, it happened by accident, but that doesn't mean you shouldn't choose the route of an entrepreneur if it fits your skillsets.

Side note: I often wonder if I would have ever gone down this route without that pressure, if I wasn't kicked out of the nest. One thing I do know is that entrepreneurs perform best under fire.

☐ 249 MENTORING

A person with ADHD is not naturally empathetic. Empathy is something the ADHD brain doesn't pick up on. There's something about the ADHD brain that only allows itself to be present in its current place in time, and not anywhere else—we become empathetic only after we've experienced something.

Hence, preparing for the future is one of our weak points. The ADHD brain cannot see three feet in front of it, but once the ADHD brain has experienced something, it locks it in. We learn the hard way, but boy do we learn.

These experiences that we learn from are pulled apart, diagrammed, and charted on a map (in our minds) for the next time we come across it, or see someone close to us going through it or getting ready to go through it. This makes us great mentors.

Do you have ADHD? If so, you should mentor someone.

☐ 250   NO AND GO

B2B—I want to talk to both sides today.

To sales people selling to business: TAKE NO

If you get a "no" then take it. A no is a no. Get out of there. It's just a waste of time, gas money, effort, energy, interest, and friendship. A no is a no.

To business owners that get approached by us, sales people, all the time: SAY NO

I've been on both sides of the coin. I know how it goes. You're just trying to be nice. As a business owner, especially as someone who understands the sales side and how hard people are working, it's so difficult sometimes to say no. Do I really want your water dispenser in my office? No, definitely not. But what we say is, "Hey, can come back and talk to me tomorrow?" Hey, business owners, just say no. You're not going to hurt anybody's feelings. True sales people will take that no and get the hell out because they know that the next yes is just around the corner.

Say no; take no; and go.

FINAL THOUGHT

You did it! You finished my book. My goal with this book was to help you get to the next level. I hope it helped you gain a deeper understanding of yourself. I hope it encouraged you to start a business, grow a business, or talked you out of starting your business.

Now what? I wrote this book to share my experiences in the hope that readers can learn from my failures and successes. Please share this book with those close to you in small business, then start sharing your experiences too. It will add more value to your failures and successes.

One last thing:

I'm here for you. I believe in you. Let me know how I can help you.

Chip@perkbird.com

C: 503-689-2366

ACKNOWLEDGEMENTS

First and foremost, thank you to my backers. This book was self-published through Kickstarter and couldn't have happened without the love, support, and harder in cash of the following people:

Ryan Gelbrich	Vicki Barram	Mike Atkinson
Leslie Buckendorf	Steve Barram	Jason Brandt
Corey Benson	Mark Anderson	Benjamin Winter
Bob Crimmins	Andrew	Ann Varelia
Kyle Sexton	Michael Roth	Chris Brickell
Dana heuberger	Dustin Namirr	Dustin Mitchell
Taylor Mutch	Stacy Spahr	Nick Gunn
Nathan Knottingham	Leslie Venti	Nick Schomus
Rob	Josh Babcock	Daniel Walker
Tom Hoffert	Nathan Boderman	Thubten
Jerry Crane	Katherine	Consciousness
Michael Hill	Jeremy Golar	Chad Kerlegan
Dean Craig	Mike Peterson	Bobby Hooper
Elaine Gesik	Rick day	Victoria Darling
Brad Sund	RJ Flake	Eric Zimmett
JLynnJohnston	Matthew Rawlins	Melissa Woodward
Brian Hart	Nathan Murray	M. Phani Sasank
Rick Turoczy	Zack Nielsen	Colby Martin
Tiffany Bulgin	Jereme Morris	Phillip & Tim Wade
Alex Casebeer	John Harvey	Tom Rooney
Kyle Borges	Mark Grimes	Crystal
Jesse Liebman	Evelyn Sabino	Dave Pluist
Damaris Diez Stevens	Anna Barram	

Special thanks for inspiration and support to Kyle Sexton, and Joy Dickenson for inspiring me to write this book. Thank you to my team at Co.W Industries and my team at Perkbird. Thanks to my editor, Denise Chin, for making me sound so smart. Thanks to Nick Pritchett for doing the cover art even before I said I would pay him to do so.

Thank you to Dr. Captain. I did it, just like you said I would.

Thanks to my friends and family for supporting me and my crazy dreams. Thanks to my mom for being my number one fan. Thank you to my kids for dealing with a dad who is slightly insane.

Thanks to my wife Jill Conrad who's made countless sacrifices so that I can continue to take risks. I don't know where I'd be without your love, support, and amazing credit…I love you.

ABOUT THE AUTHOR

Chip Conrad is a husband, father, and serial entrepreneur. He is the cofounder of a start-up called Perkbird, and Co.W, co-working space located in Salem, Oregon. Chip is president of the Center for Entrepreneurial Education and Development, a nonprofit he started to help teach young people how to start and run their own company. He also spends much of his time consulting and speaking on the subject of small business. This is Chip's first book.

Made in the USA
San Bernardino, CA
06 January 2017